JIM THORPE

ORIGINAL ALL-AMERICAN

Jim Thorpe, 1912

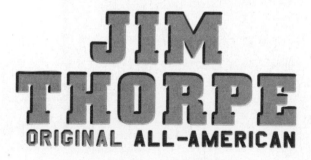

JIM THORPE
ORIGINAL ALL-AMERICAN

JOSEPH BRUCHAC

Dial Books / Walden Media®

DIAL BOOKS
A member of Penguin Group (USA) Inc.
Published by The Penguin Group
Penguin Group (USA) Inc., 375 Hudson Street, New York, NY 10014, U.S.A.

Penguin Group (Canada), 90 Eglinton Avenue East, Suite 700, Toronto, Ontario,
Canada M4P 2Y3 (a division of Pearson Penguin Canada Inc.)
Penguin Books Ltd, 80 Strand, London WC2R 0RL, England
Penguin Ireland, 25 St. Stephen's Green, Dublin 2, Ireland
(a division of Penguin Books Ltd)
Penguin Group (Australia), 250 Camberwell Road, Camberwell, Victoria 3124,
Australia (a division of Pearson Australia Group Pty Ltd)
Penguin Books India Pvt Ltd, 11 Community Centre, Panchsheel Park,
New Delhi - 110 017, India
Penguin Group (NZ), Cnr Airborne and Rosedale Roads, Albany, Auckland 1310,
New Zealand (a division of Pearson New Zealand Ltd)
Penguin Books (South Africa) (Pty) Ltd, 24 Sturdee Avenue, Rosebank,
Johannesburg 2196, South Africa
Penguin Books Ltd, Registered Offices: 80 Strand, London WC2R 0RL, England

This book is published in partnership with Walden Media, LLC. Walden Media and
the Walden Media skipping stone logo are trademarks and registered trademarks of
Walden Media, LLC, 294 Washington Street, Boston, Massachusetts 02108.

The publisher does not have any control over and does not assume any
responsibility for author or third-party websites or their content.

All photographs are courtesy of the
Cumberland County Historical Society, Carlisle, PA.

Designed by Nancy R. Leo-Kelly
Text set in Trump Mediaeval
Printed in the U.S.A.
1 3 5 7 9 10 8 6 4 2

Library of Congress Cataloging-in-Publication Data
Bruchac, Joseph, date.
Jim Thorpe : original All-American / Joseph Bruchac.
p. cm.
ISBN 0-8037-3118-3
1. Thorpe, Jim, 1887–1953—Juvenile literature.
2. Athletes—United States—Biography—Juvenile literature.
3. Indian athletes—United States—Biography—Juvenile literature. I. Title.
GV697.T5B77 2006   796.092—dc22

*This story is dedicated to
the grandchildren of all those who were sent
to Carlisle and to all those who ran.*

CONTENTS

The 1911 season has brought into the public eye a young Indian student at the Carlisle School who promises to be the greatest athlete the world has ever seen. James Thorpe, a Sac and Fox from Oklahoma, came to Carlisle in 1908 with no knowledge whatsoever of athletics. The world of college trainers has been astonished by his achievements. He is not only a basketball player, at which game he fills the center post with truly remarkable skill, but he is a baseball player of great talent and covers any of the sacks or outfields with as much credit as a professional. He can put the 16 pound shot 43 feet, runs 100 in 10 seconds, while the 220 hurdles he negotiates in 26 seconds. The high hurdles are pie for him in 15 4/5 seconds, while the 220 hurdles he negotiates in 26 seconds. The youthful redskin hunts, plays lacrosse, tennis, indoor baseball, handball, hockey all with equal skill and can fill almost any position on a football team with superlative credit.

— from the Muskogee *Times-Democrat*
November 1911

1

YOU CAN CALL ME JIM

You can call me Jim. I've had other names, some good, some bad. Some of them I've accepted and some I have fought against. But Jim, well, that's the one my pa gave when he first looked at me and my twin brother, Charlie.

James Francis Thorpe, he said. That is what we are going to name him.

Thinking back on it, he could have done a whole lot worse. At least he didn't call me after his own pa, my Irish grandfather, like he'd been named. Then I would have been Hiram Thorpe the Third.

James Francis Thorpe wasn't bad at all. Ma had other ideas, though. She had in mind what she had seen when she looked outside our cabin there in Indian Territory that May afternoon in 1887 when I was born. And when an Indian woman has something in mind, she generally gets her way. A lot of

Indians get their name from something their mother saw right after they were born. Like my friend named Two Dogs. Just kidding.

But Ma was not just kidding. That image of the sun lighting up the walkway leading away from the door was strong in her mind.

"His name is Wathohuck," she said. "Bright Path."

And that surely is a good name, too.

What were those other names I got called?

My brother. That was one of the very best of them.

"Wait for me, my brother!"

Charlie would call those words out to me when we were running across the plains chasing after jackrabbits or going up our favorite hill, him trying hard to keep up with me. And I always stopped to wait for him to catch up. I don't think there's anyone in life who ever comes closer to a person than his twin brother. We were always together. We're together now. And I hope you understand what I mean when I say that.

Stupid. That was what the teacher called me. And not just one teacher, either.

Stupid. I hated that name. That was one of the worst ones. Not the very worst, but close. It hurt so much because I wondered if it was true. When it came to book learning I was painful slow. I had always been the swift one when it came to outdoors things, the first to learn how to make and shoot a bow, to ride a horse. (When I was on a horse's back I understood

Jim, age three, with his twin brother, Charles

what some of our old men meant when they said us Sac and Fox could almost forgive the white man for the bad that was done to us seeing as how he also brought us the gift of horses.) Charlie, though, was the one who dashed ahead when we got sent off to the mission school at the age of six.

Just looking at all those strange twisty shapes crawling across the white pages, those letters and numbers like little black insects—it gave me a head-ache. The pictures weren't so bad, but there wasn't ever enough of them.

"You can do it, Jim." That is what my brother Charlie would say.

And because he believed in me, I finally did. I learned to read and to write—better than any of those teachers ever thought I could. I even got so I could cipher, though it was hard to make real sense out of all the numbers, which didn't tell stories like words could do.

School, I never loved it, but I would have done any-thing for Charlie. Maybe, if he had stayed, I would have learned to like it better. But he didn't. When the influenza burned through the school that second winter like a fire out of control in the prairie grass, it took Charlie with it.

And I took to running away from that awful place. Even though I was small back then—I didn't get my growth until real late—they were never able to catch me. Just as long as I had a home to go to, I always got back home.

And Pa always had the same thing to say. Some-times he was angry when he said it, sometimes he was just resigned.

"You're going back."

Pa had his way about that, just as Ma had hers about my Indian name. Not that she disagreed with him about my needing education. Both of them had seen how Indians were cheated by white men who

4

knew more about such things as book learning. Being cheated was how we Sac and Fox had ended up way down in Oklahoma, far from the lands where our people used to live near the big freshwater seas. We'd been cheated so often by the whites that finally great chief Black Hawk fought back hard in a war that scared the pants off the United States back in 1832. Black Hawk and his men pushed back across the Mississippi and defeated the army and drove all the way up into Wisconsin before they finally got outnumbered and outgunned and had to surrender.

Pa was always proud of Black Hawk. He made sure that all his kids knew about him and shared that pride. No-ten-o-quah, my father's mother, was from Black Hawk's own Thunder Clan, so our family felt as if we were Black Hawk's family. My mother even used to say that she thought I was Black Hawk come back to life again. I was born to do great things. My destiny was not to be the same kind of warrior Black Hawk was, but I would fight in my own way for Indian people.

Even though he was beat in war, Black Hawk never gave in. Once they'd released him from captivity, he spoke up and told the Indian side of things to reporters. His story even got published in a book, and I think that was one of the reasons Pa wanted all his children to be able to read. That way they could read Black Hawk's story for themselves.

Not that reading was the only way I could learn about Black Hawk. When I was a boy there was plenty of Sac and Fox men willing to tell the stories of that war to any child ready to listen. And they would tell them in our language and not in that English which was the only thing we was allowed to speak in the mission school. A few of the oldest men were actual veterans of that war, and as for the others, well their fathers and grandfathers had fought by old Black Hawk's side. Being away at school so much meant I never got enough chances to listen to those stories. I still regret that.

Pa's own knowledge of reading and writing had, I must admit, served him in good stead. We had our own place and there was always enough for Pa and Ma to feed my other brothers and sisters. Even in Oklahoma, there were still more than enough dishonest white men who would cheat an Indian out of everything he owned.

"You're going back," Pa would say.

I begged him. And Ma, too. She let her eyes be kinder as she looked at me, but she shook her head. I think it was because she knew that path in her vision had led *away* from our door. I had to make my way out into the world. Even though I was stubborn enough to keep fighting against it.

Stubborn. I have been called that plenty often, too. I'll accept that name.

RUNNING AWAY

Thinking back on it, you might say that running was what brought me to football. By that I mean running away from school. After Charlie died, the Sac and Fox Indian Agency School was the last place on earth I wanted to be. I begged to stay home, but Pa said I needed book learning. So back I went.

Book learning. That was far from the only thing I had to do. All of my time at that school wasn't just spent at a desk. They had to keep the costs low and couldn't afford much help. So us students had to do just about all the labor. They had us peeling potatoes, chopping wood and lugging water for the cook, washing our clothes under the watchful eye of the laundress, growing most of the food we ate in the school gardens, mucking out the stables, and cleaning the outhouses.

Now, I was used to hard work. I was glad to do my share of it at home on our ranch. But I resented having to do all those jobs in a school where they never praised you and would just as soon whup you as criticize you. They did plenty of both.

Talk about discipline. Everything there was done by the bell. Whenever that bell rang, you had to move! We got up by the bell, ate by the bell, went to class by the bell, sung the words in *Gospel Hymns* # 5 by the bell. And we didn't just walk from one place to the next, they marched us like stiff little soldiers.

Even playtime—or so they called it—was done by the bell. But we weren't allowed to play the kind of games we all knew as Indian kids. No dart games of mis-qua-pee, or follow the leader or even tag. Instead they made us play horseshoes—probably because it was one game that required us just to stand in one place—until that danged bell rang again. If they could have made us go to the bathroom by the bell they would have done that. To this day, whenever I hear a bell it makes me want to run the other way.

There was about sixty of us, boys and girls. Most of us were Sac and Fox, but there were a few Potawatomis, Kickapoos, Iowas, and even some Ottawas. None of us was that happy to be there. Some of those unhappy children were "blanket Indians" whose families had never spoken English before. Those of us who came from mixed-blood families like mine, where English was spoken, had to act as translators for those boys and girls. We had to tell them that not only had their clothes been taken away and their long hair cut off, but now they didn't even have the same names they came there with. Instead of Chi-ki-ka, she was now Stella. Instead of Keokuk, he was now Robert.

We all felt like scarecrows in the clothes they forced us into. We boys wore government issue coats that were made out of thick black cloth. They usually were two sizes too big so we would grow into them. Our heads were weighted down with black felt hats and our necks were strangled with those cheviot shirts with collars as tight as a noose. We even had to wear vests! I was always too hot in those clothes and I couldn't wait to take them off at night. I couldn't hardly imagine how trapped and lost those other kids must have felt. They had grown up on the prairie, wearing soft and comfortable old-style Indian clothes. The kind of "civilization" we had been shoved into must have made them feel like muskrats with their legs in a steel trap.

At night, as I lay in my narrow cot in the boys' dormitory, I could hear some of them crying softly. Now and then, as they slept, I think they'd escape for a time in their dreams. They'd speak out a word or two in our language that made me know they thought they was back home with their families. But if they spoke those words too loud, they might be heard by one of the teachers who monitored us even when we slept. Then they'd be woken up and whupped for talking something other than English. So they couldn't even get away in their dreams.

I felt sad about those "poor uncivilized" boys and girls (as Superintendent Wagner called them), but it was even sadder for me to see their parents. In those days, Indian parents didn't have any choice about what happened to their kids as far as education went. If the government said their children had to go to school, that was it. No explanation, no discussion. The Indian agent would just load them in the wagon and away they'd go.

Those parents had their children taken away from them and couldn't quite understand what this whole school thing meant. Five or six families had followed their children to the school. Since they weren't allowed to stay on the grounds, they had set up camp along the creek by the Sac and Fox Agency so that they could at least see their children now and then. Seeing those sad-faced blanket Indians down by the creek made me miss my own home that much more.

All I could think of was our ranch, twenty-three miles away. It didn't matter if I was sitting in the classroom or working in the harness shop, my heart and my thoughts were at home with Ma and Pa and my little brothers and sisters. I thought of those new colts that needed to be broke. I wondered how the cattle were doing or if the hogs had broken out of their sty again. Maybe there was fence that needed mending. There were twelve hundred acres on our allotment. Pa needed all the help he could get around the ranch.

One day, out of the corner of my eye, I took notice of the fact that my industrial teacher had his back turned. The next thing I knew, I was already half-way home. Of course, like I said before, Pa insisted I had to go back. First he whupped me, just so I would remember what he'd said. Then he hitched the wagon, loaded me in, and drove the twenty-three miles back to the school, where he dropped me off at the gate. But he neglected to tell me I should stay there. As soon as he was over the hill, I took off running across lots. That cut about five miles off the distance home. I got back there just the same time as my father did.

I did that more than once.

"Keep this up, son," Pa said, "and I promise I shall send you so far away to school, you won't be able to run home."

I kept it up and he kept his promise. That was why, in the fall of 1898 when I was just eleven years old, I found myself arriving at the new Haskell Indian Junior College in Lawrence, Kansas. It was 270 miles away from our allotment acres on the North Canadian River, so there was no way I'd be running all that way home. Or so Pa thought.

THE FINEST GAME IN THE WORLD

It had been a long trip to get to Haskell. First there had been the thirty-mile wagon ride up to Guthrie along the dusty Indian Territory roads. From there I'd taken my first train ride north to Arkansas City just across the Kansas line, where I was loaded onto another train that took me through Kansas City to my final destination, up in the northeastern corner of the state. It was country I'd never seen before, but I had a good sense of where I was in relation to where I'd been. I had been keeping an eye on where the sun was in the sky, just like Pa had taught me to do when we were out hunting.

It was September 17 when I got out on the platform at Lawrence. I looked back over my shoulder down the tracks that led to the southwest. That way was home. I looked in front of me, across the flat plain where a building that looked as large as a hill loomed over the landscape. That way was where I was going, at least for now.

One of the first things they did was cut off my hair. That was not as much a trial to me as I am sure it must have been to those wilder Indian boys who'd never cut their hair their entire lives. Being from a more civilized family, I was used to wearing my hair short. But in most Indian families, even among my own Sac and Fox people, it was just about a sacred thing for a man to have long hair.

In some ways, Haskell was just more of the same. Just like at our Sac and Fox school there was marching and bells, and just about all of the hard work in the world being done by the Indian students. But it was different, too. One difference was how big it was. There wasn't just four or five tribes here with most of the students being Sac and Fox. Here at Haskell there were a thousand students from ninety different tribes. I'd never seen so many Indians in one place before.

There was a band, too, that played while the students were marching. That marching and drilling was darn good. It was exciting to watch company after company of Indians in spiffy uniforms turning on a dime and coming to attention. The uniforms at Haskell were all cut to fit because they were made by the Indian students themselves in the tailor shop. The brass buttons reflected the sunlight like little fires and the boots was all spit polished so that they shone like glass. When I was issued my own uniform you can bet that I kept it neat and ironed. It wasn't just because we had inspection every Saturday and could get punished if everything wasn't exactly right. I liked the way I looked in those new clothes and being part of those marching ranks, moving in perfect unison, felt good. It was slick! Before long I could snap out a salute with the best of them and my feet was never out of step.

Our days were kept busy. Every morning we spent four hours in the classroom. It was mostly grammar and composition, American history, and mathematics. Then in the afternoons we were assigned to the trade shops to learn a vocation. Those shops included ones for such things as blacksmithing, baking, tailoring, even wagon building. And they were not meant just for teaching but also for production. The superintendent of Haskell was proud of the fact that the year before I'd come, their wagon shop had turned out fifty farm wagons and five spring wagons. You'd only be assigned to a shop for six months at a time. Then you'd be rotated to another trade to find out what you was best at doing.

There's some things about Haskell I will never forget. The prairie stretched out wide and lonesome around us. When the bugle call sounded for us to assemble, it just echoed out for miles. We would all run to come to attention there in front of the big four-story gray stone building that was our dormitory. Then we would march by companies to the dining hall.

Un-cover would come the command and we'd whip off our military caps and snap to attention while the school band played "The Star-Spangled Banner." Then we'd march in to our tables to stand behind our chairs and sing a hymn before we could sit down to eat. The food there wasn't anything like my ma's wonderful cooking. It was mostly just unbuttered bread, potatoes, hominy, and now and then, as if by accident, a little meat. But at least there was plenty of it, unlike the Sac and Fox school, where we'd gone to bed hungry more than a few times.

Reveille, which was the wake-up bugle call, was at 5:45 A.M. Taps, which meant it was time to go to bed, was at 9 P.M. Every day was like that and every day was filled with schoolwork and labor and marching and bugles and bells and penalties for everything from talking Indian to failing to make your bed right. But there was also time just about every day for something that they never had at the Sac and Fox school. There was time to play and practice real sports. They had baseball and track.

They also had something called basketball. Back then, that was a real new sport, that game of bouncing a round ball and then throwing it up so that it fell through a basket. It had only been invented seven years earlier and the baskets that was used were sometimes just that, bushel baskets with the bottoms cut out, nailed up to a backboard. New as the game was, our Haskell basketball players were no slouches. Our boys beat teams like the University of Kansas. In fact, Dr. James Naismith himself, who invented the game, was a teacher at Haskell.

Best of all, though, was another game I had never seen or heard of before. It was called football. I loved it from the first moment I saw it.

Since Charlie's death I'd felt so alone that I had held back from making friends and playing with other boys my age. But here at Haskell, farther away from home than I'd ever imagined I would be, I started making

15

friends. Sports was part of it. I was one of the small boys who spent as much free time as was allowed out on the sidelines watching the football team practice and trying to copy our heroes. My favorite player was Chauncy Archiquette, the star halfback.

Football had only come to Haskell two years before, but our team was already real good. They played a schedule of six games, which was all they could get. It was hard for the other teams, none of which was all-Indian like ours, to keep up with us. All of us had been running and playing rough games since we were little, so we were always stronger and in better shape than most of those non-Indian teams. And I think some of them were afraid of us because we were "wild Indians." No college teams would agree to play Haskell, except for Purdue, which scheduled not just one game with Haskell that fall of '98 but two.

I was far too small for football then. I was just under five feet tall and weighed 106 pounds. Another Indian boy named Henry Roberts, who was my same age and size, was always there watching with me. We made up a ball of our own, an old sock stuffed with grass, and the two of us gathered some of the other boys together to play a game on the sidelines.

One day, as we were playing in our work shirts, jeans, and heavy shoes, I managed to break through the tackles of the other boys and cross our improvised goal line.

"Archiquette scores again," I yelled, surprising

even myself. I was quiet and shy in those days and my shout had been a lot louder than I'd intended.

"Is that so?" said an amused voice from behind me. I turned to look up at the smiling face of none other than Chauncy Archiquette himself. I couldn't smile back, though. I was too embarrassed to even move.

"Let me see what you're using for a ball," he said. I managed to raise the hand that held the sock stuffed with grass.

Archiquette took the pathetic attempt at a football from me, tossed it up into the air, then flipped it over toward Henry. Henry didn't even try to catch it. He just let it bounce off him onto the ground.

"What's your name?" Chauncy asked me.

"JimThorpesir," I croaked.

"Come on, JimThorpesir," Chauncy Archiquette said, his smile a little broader as he patted me on my shoulder. "Walk with me and tell me what you know about football."

I couldn't feel my legs move, but somehow I kept up with him. As we walked I told him what I'd learned from watching their practices. My voice wasn't much more than a whisper, but Chauncy nodded as I described the different positions from quarterback to lineman, how the man running with the ball was supposed to avoid being tackled by the other team, what downs were and touchdowns and how you could also score by kicking a ball through the goalposts.

Pretty soon we were standing in front of the harness shop, where Chauncy had his work assignment.

"You learned all that by watching?" he asked me.

"Yes sir," I said, saluting as I did so.

That salute made Chauncy laugh out loud. "At ease," he said. "Come inside with me."

We went into the harness shop, a place I'd not yet worked. There was tools and leather everywhere. It smelled like the tack room in our barn back home. No one paid any attention to me because I was with Chauncy, who they nodded and smiled at. As Haskell's best athlete, he got special treatment wherever he went. Chauncy grabbed a couple pieces of leather, put a padded glove on his hand, and picked up a needle. Almost in no time at all he had sewed together a football that he stuffed with rags. Then he gave it to me.

"A boy knows as much about the finest game in the world as you do oughta have a football of their own," he said.

4

CARLISLE'S VISIT

Once I had a football of my own, I organized a team of boys my own age and we played regular games against each other. I used every play I saw on the field. Sometimes I was the quarterback, but my favorite position was halfback. I loved it when I had the ball. Even though my legs were short, I was the fastest runner on our little team.

Not just Chauncy, but also some of the other big guys on the school team started to take notice of me.

"Jim," they'd say, "when you get your growth, you could be some kind of a player."

Although I also learned how to play baseball and basketball, football stayed my favorite. That's one reason why I got so excited about the rumor that went around the school one January day.

My friend Henry Roberts passed it on to me when we sat by each other at breakfast.

"The Carlisle Indians are a-coming," he said, not looking at me as he spoke and keeping his voice low.

"Carlisle?" I said. "You sure?" I was so excited that my voice got louder than I meant it to and I turned toward Henry, almost knocking over my cup.

"Thorpe!" barked the disciplinarian who had just come up to stand behind me without me noticing. I recognized his voice. It was Washington, one of the senior boys who was known to hand out penalties pretty freely. "Yes sir," I said, turning my attention back to my plate and waiting to hear what my punishment was going to be for speaking out like that at the table. Instead, though, he just walked on. Now that I think of it, he was probably as excited about that rumor as me and Henry was. That was probably why he let my misbehavior slide.

The thought of the Carlisle Indians actually coming to Haskell was thrilling to all of us. Could it really be true?

The Carlisle Indians weren't a tribe, but they were real Indians, all right, and they were our heroes. They were the football team from the United States Indian Industrial School in Carlisle, Pennsylvania. The best football team of all.

You have to understand that back then, just at the end of the ninteenth century, Indians didn't have many heroes left. All of our great leaders had been killed or defeated in battle. What little land we had left was shrinking and so, too, were our numbers. The popular wisdom was that Indians were a dying breed. The only hope we had for survival, and it was a slim hope at that, was to give up everything that was Indian and to try to be white men. Well, not exactly white men. If we were "lucky," we could be good enough to work for white men as laborers and servants and tradesmen. Most people—including a lot of Indians, I am sorry to say—believed that white people were just naturally better than all the other races. If you *didn't* believe it, all you had to do was pick up a newspaper or a magazine and see what it had to say. I'd finally learned to read pretty well by the middle of my first year at Haskell. It just made me feel sick sometimes to read what they said about Indians, about how uncivilized and weak and hopeless we all were.

But then there was the Carlisle Indians. They were so strong, they beat the best white college teams. It was like all the old warriors, Geronimo and Sitting Bull and Pontiac and Osceola and Black Hawk, had come back to life in those young men from all the different tribes who stepped out onto the football field to do battle. They made us proud.

The Carlisle Indians here? It didn't seem possible. But the rumor turned out to be true. They had just played a game against the University of California, farther than any football team had ever gone to play another. And even though it took them a week and a half to get there, they'd still managed to squeak out a victory.

Carlisle was sort of the granddaddy of all the Indian schools in the United States, the most famous of them all. Haskell had been designed on the Carlisle model and was regarded as the second-best Indian school. So a visit to Haskell on the way back was a natural thing to do.

On January 12, the Carlisle team got off the train. The whole student body was lined up and waiting for them. Our feet thudded like a thousand drumbeats on the earth as we marched by in a full-dress parade before they had breakfast with us, sitting at the head table in the domestic science hall.

Supervisor Wright was almost giddy when he got up to welcome our guests.

"Today," he said, "we bring together Carlisle and Haskell, the two best schools in the Indian Service, the two best schools in the United States. Today I have seen the best thing at Carlisle and the best thing at Haskell—the Carlisle football team and the cooking class at Haskell Institute."

I was lucky enough that day to have been one of the students assigned to be a waiter. So I got to walk right up to the Carlisle table and stand next to every one of those great players. They were all wearing their red turtlenecks with a big *C* on the front. The first one to catch my eye was Thaddeus Redwater. He was six feet four inches tall and towered over everyone else, even when he was sitting down. He was from the Cheyenne Indian Reservation in Montana and played end. Dwarfed by him was the team's quarterback, Frank Hudson, who was a Pueblo Indian from New Mexico. Hudson was only five feet five inches tall and was also the team's kicker. Seeing someone that small on such a great team gave me hope. If I could just grow another six inches I'd be his height.

Across from them were my favorites, the running backs. They were the team's two Iroquois All-Americans. Martin Wheelock, an Oneida, was a second-team All-American, and he sat next to Isaac Seneca, whose open field running had earned him a slot as a first-team All-American.

What would it be like to be one of them? Before, I'd only dreamed about growing up enough to play football for Haskell. Now I had a different dream. I wanted to be a Carlisle Indian.

BACK HOME

I still missed home plenty. The memories of what it was like would come back to me at night sometimes. I'd think about riding horses or being out hunting with my bow and arrows. There was none of that at Haskell, just drilling and studying and work. If it wasn't for the sports, I would have burst.

All I had of home was memories. They came to me all the time. I'd be sitting in the dining hall and I'd see myself back there at the table, with Pa at the head and Ma at the other end and my sisters Mary and Rosetta and Adaline and my baby brother. That would make me smile until I would think about how I hardly knew the littlest ones. I had been away at school most of their lives. Rosetta was five, Adaline was only three, and little Eddie had just been born not long before I was sent off to Kansas.

Or I might call to mind my older brothers George and Frank, who were not at home but off at the Sac and Fox school. I'd never been that close to George, but I'd looked up to my half brother Frank—even when he teased me and said things like "Jim, you ever going to grow taller? You're so little you need a stepladder to comb your hair."

Other times I would find myself working in the wagon shop and it would take me back to the chores I did with Pa around the ranch. Or I would go past the kitchen and smell the bread and I'd see Ma's hands holding out one of her new-baked loaves.

I don't mean to say things was perfect back home. Pa and Ma always fought some. I could understand why they might quarrel. Life was hard. It wasn't just the work we all had to do, either. It was hard to bear the losses. Charlie wasn't the only one who died young. Before we was even born, Ma had twin daughters who had passed when they were babies.

Another of those losses to our family came while I was at Haskell. A letter arrived telling me that Rosetta had died of a fever. For weeks after that I walked around in a daze, wondering if I ever would see any of my family again in this world. I dreaded the thought of getting another letter like that.

But I stuck it out at Haskell more than halfway through 1901. It was late summer and I was walking across the field when one of my classmates came running up to me.

"Jim," he said, "there's a letter for you in the school office. Your pa's been in a hunting accident and got shot in the chest. Money is being sent so you can take the train home."

I hardly heard those last words of his. I never did find out why they didn't give that letter to me right away. I just took off on my own. I didn't change out of my work clothes or pack a bag. I just turned around and started running. I climbed over the fence and lit out for the railroad yards in Lawrence. I didn't have a cent on me, but I saw any empty boxcar in a freight train being made up. From what it said on the side, Ottawa–Kansas City, I figured it was going south. I remembered passing through Ottawa, Kansas, on my way to Haskell on the train. I was inside that boxcar when it rolled out of the yard.

Later that afternoon, when the train slowed to a stop, the door of the boxcar rolled open and a brakeman looked in at me.

"Hop on out of there," he said. "We don't allow no riders."

"Sir," I said, "I got to get home to Oklahoma Territory. My pa's been hurt."

The man shook his head. "Son," he said, "in that case you better get down for sure. You're going the wrong way. This train's headed north."

I got off that train fast and started walking. I decided there'd be no more trains. From then on I had to stick to the roads. I'd find a place to curl up at night, sleep a little, and then wake and start off again, heading south by the sun. Since it was summer, it wasn't that hard to find food to eat and there were friendly folks along the way who didn't mind helping out an Indian boy with no money. When my feet got tired, I hitched rides on ox-drawn freighters and wagons pulled by horses. All in all, it took me the better part of two weeks to get home.

When I walked into our front yard, what I saw

made me both happy and worried at the same time. There on the front stoop sat Pa. He was a bit thin, but healthy looking. He had made a full recovery from that gunshot wound. I could tell by the look on his face that he was glad to see me but trying not to show it.

What worried me was the willow stick he was holding in his hand. I knew what that was for. He'd gotten the word from Haskell about my running off without waiting for the money to take the train. I had made up my mind as I traveled that 270 miles back home.

"I'm not going back," I said. Being bullheaded is one of the characteristics of our clan.

"Yes, you are," Pa said, his face darkening with anger.

"Nope."

Pa wore out that stick on me. I didn't like it, but I accepted it. Then he tried talking. That didn't work, either. Ma was expecting again and not feeling so well. The only one at home to help Pa out with the chores was my brother George. I was fourteen now. Even though I was still small, I was strong and able as any grown man when it came to taking care of horses and cattle.

I never went back to Haskell.

6

GARDEN GROVE

For a while, things went pretty well at home. Pa needed my help around our ranch and I settled into the routine of taking care of the stock and working with the horses. I loved riding and roping, and there was time for me to do other things I'd not been able to do at school, especially hunting for the table.

I still had some problems with my pa, though. Pa was never beat in either a fistfight or a wrestling match. He also wore a pistol on his side and knew how to use it. Even when he went over to Keokuk Falls, where many a gunfight took place just like in one of those Hollywood movies I'd take part in years later, people stepped aside when they saw Hiram P. Thorpe coming.

No one outside our family dared stand up to Pa. But I guess you know who in our family was stupid and stubborn enough to do just that.

One afternoon, when we was supposed to be watching the stock, I talked George into going fishing with me. We came back with a good big string of fish, but we also found Pa waiting for us. He had found his cattle and horses scattered all over the ranch and he was as mad as a hornet.

We got a serious whupping for that. I guess I

deserved it, but I didn't like taking it. So that night I ran away from home. I had heard a man who was good with horses could find a job down on the high plains of the Texas panhandle. Sure enough, when I got to Texas, I found me a job on a ranch fixing fences and taming wild horses.

I was only fifteen. Though I had grown some I wasn't more than five feet six inches and weighed only about 140 pounds, as compared to the 1,200 pounds of a twisting, biting, bucking bronc. I took my share of falls, but I was always up and back on that horse until I rode the fight right out of it. I never met a mustang that I could not catch, saddle, and ride. That is one achievement of my boyhood days that I do not hesitate to feel proud about.

I spent a year down there along the Brazos River as a broncobuster. But I never stopped thinking of my home. I longed to see my ma, hear her voice, and taste her cooking. I missed my brothers and sisters. I even missed Pa. I saved up enough to get a fine team of horses and headed back home. When Pa saw those horses, he had to smile.

"Well," he said, "as long as you are back, I guess you can stay."

This brings me to a part of my story that it saddens me to tell. Ma gave birth to a boy who was her eleventh child. He only lived three days. It wasn't an easy birth and Ma was so weakened by it that she never recovered. When she passed two weeks later, Pa was there by her side. Ma was buried in the cem-

29

etery at Sacred Heart. There had been a fire three months before and the mission and the school there had been burned right to the ground. When I stood at Ma's grave, my heart felt like the blackened ruins of that place.

Pa married again. I didn't blame him. It was hard for a man with young children to go it alone. His new wife was named Julia Hardin, and as stepmothers go she wasn't bad. But life at home would never be the same.

A few miles up the trail from our ranch a new school had just been opened by a teacher named Walter White. It was not an Indian school, but a public one for white and Indian students alike. Pa had kept insisting that I go back to school and I finally agreed to see what Garden Grove was like.

So it was that Mr. White arrived at his school one morning to find Pa and me there waiting for him. I kept my eyes on the ground as Pa talked with him.

"Can you teach the boy anything?" Pa asked. "I take him to agency school, he come back. I take him again, he come back. Five, six, ten times I take him. All time he come back."

Mr. White turned to me. I liked him for doing that.

"Why did you leave the agency school, Jim?" he asked.

"I don't like it," I said, still looking down, but watching him out of the corner of my eye.

"Did they do things to you, punish you or things like that?"

"No," I said slowly, scuffing my toe in the soft earth. That wasn't the truth, of course. I had taken plenty of beatings, suffered under more kinds of harsh discipline than I cared to talk about. But I didn't know if this white man would believe me, despite his quiet tone. So I kept it simple. "The agency school is just not good for Indians," I said. "Indian boys don't like it."

What Mr. White said next was so simple and direct that it surprised me.

"Will you run away from this school?"

"I will not run away," I said. And I didn't.

It wasn't just that I was convinced by Mr. White's sincerity. For the first time in my life, going to school didn't mean going away. Attending school at Garden Grove meant I could come home every night. I could sleep in my own bed. I could play with my little sister and brother and go hunting and fishing on the weekends.

Of course, there was still plenty to do around our ranch. Pa made sure I knew what chores had to be done. I made sure I did them. But it was mostly the sort of work I enjoyed, a good part of it on horseback, which I truly loved. Caring for the stock, riding our fence line, I could tell that Pa liked having me there by his side working.

And it wasn't just work that we did together. When I went hunting, Pa often went with me. I never knew any man who was better in the woods than Pa. His strength was truly amazing. One time Pa and me both shot a buck. We were a good two miles away from our horses and I wasn't big enough to drag a deer myself. So Pa picked up both deer, slung one over each shoulder, and lugged them back to the horses without even breathing hard.

Pa's strength also showed at what he called his "amateur track meets," which were held at our place on weekends and holidays. It's an old, old tradition among the Sac and Fox to get the men together to run races, see who can jump the farthest, and have wrestling matches. One of the first stories Pa ever told me about Black Hawk was that he'd been the greatest runner of all and no one ever threw him in wrestling. Being home meant I could watch Pa and the other men engaging in those contests of power and speed. Just like our clan ancestor old Chief Black Hawk, no one was ever able to defeat Pa.

We boys had our own little contests, imitating the grown-ups. Even though I was still small for my age I could outrun and outjump them all. I even got the better of some of the bigger boys when it came to grappling.

There was sports at Garden Grove, too. Our little school was a far cry from Haskell, but it still had its share of athletics. One of them was baseball. Around home, with my friends, we'd played our own version of the game, using sticks for bats and round stones for balls, making up rules as we went along. Mr. White, though, had raised money to buy regulation balls and bases, bats, and gloves. What we played at Garden Grove was the real thing.

Mr. White also laid out a track and rigged up a pit and bars for a high jump and pole vault. As soon as that high jump was set up, a bunch of the boys gave it a try.

Before long they were clearing four feet and then five as they moved the bar higher. I'd seen people high-jumping when I was at Haskell, but was too little then to try it myself, although I did practice by jumping over the wire fences around the school. Since coming home I'd kept on doing that. I would never walk around to a gate when I came to one of those chest-high four-strand barbed wire fences. I'd just leap it from a standstill.

I was now seven inches taller than I'd been at Haskell. Clearing that high jump bar at Garden Grove looked like something I could do. But I hung back, just watching out of the corner of my eye. I wanted to study it a bit more.

Mr. White noticed me and called me over.

"Jim," he said, "why don't you try that?"

"Sure," I said.

I ambled over, took a little run, and cleared it with inches to spare. They kept moving it up until I was jumping over my own head—higher than any of the taller boys could go.

When school ended that summer, Mr. White and some of the folks in the nearby town of Bellemont decided to organize a baseball team. Bellemont had done quite a bit of growing since the turn of the century. What had just been a crossroads with a store and a stable now had a population of close to 150 people. When that Bellemont team got put together, Mr. White made sure that I was on it. We went up against small-time teams from other towns around us. I pitched, played outfield, and got plenty of hits when I was at bat. No one was better at running the bases than me.

Our Bellemont boys seldom lost. Mr. White said I was the main part of that, being the best baseball player he had ever seen. Whether that was true or not, word did get around. That may have been why, in the fall of 1904, a recruiter from Carlisle came to visit.

7

OFF TO CARLISLE

It was no accident that the Carlisle Indian Industrial School had great sports teams. The school made an active effort at finding and recruiting the very best Indian runners and baseball players and football players. Carlisle had contacts throughout the Indian Service, the federal organization that handled all the U.S. government's dealings with the various tribes. Teachers and Indian agents regularly passed on the word to the Carlisle coaches about promising Native boys who might become part of the great Carlisle sports machine.

The man who came to Garden Grove School was an assistant superintendent at Carlisle who was traveling around the Oklahoma and Indian Territories to look at some of those prospective candidates.

Mr. White looked pleased as Punch when he introduced the man to me.

"Young Thorpe here," Mr. White said, "is a natural athlete. He can play any position on a baseball team, and when it comes to running and jumping, I have never seen his like."

"How would you like to be a Carlisle man?" the recruiter asked me.

I was sixteen years old then, and I'd been doing

35

some thinking about what life would be like for me if I just stayed around home. Ma was gone. My brother George had moved away. Pa had remarried and his new wife was expecting another baby. Even though I would always love the red earth of Oklahoma, home was not the same anymore. Our cedar cabin was starting to feel too small for me. I needed more of a challenge in my life.

So I asked that recruiter a question.

"Can I study electricity at Carlisle?" I'd been hearing more and more about the new electrical trade and it seemed like something I might want to get into.

The man paused a moment, then he put a big smile on his face. "Son," he said, "let me tell you. You can study just about any trade at Carlisle."

I thought about that. I had dreamed about being a Carlisle Indian when I was at Haskell. Sure, it was another faraway Indian school. I figured it would be just like every other Indian school in a lot of ways—filled with homesick children from many tribes, torn away from their families, forbidden to speak their language, most of them wanting to be anywhere but there. This time, though, I wouldn't be a little kid but a young man who'd seen something of the world. This time I had some idea of what to expect. From my time at Haskell, I already knew what it was like to have my hair cut short, to wear a uniform, to get up to the sound of a bugle and march to class. But at Carlisle I also just might have a chance to be on that great Carlisle football team.

Wouldn't it be grand, I thought, if I could actually be one of those players?

It wasn't a foolish thought. I had done some growing since leaving Haskell. I was only about five feet six inches, a little small for football, but I could catch up soon. Plus there would be other sports at Carlisle I'd be plenty big enough for, especially track and baseball. It wouldn't be easy. I knew that for sure. But I was the son of Hiram Thorpe. A challenge had never scared me. And I couldn't imagine any place in the world where I would be more challenged than at a big-time sports school such as Carlisle.

"Yes," I said. "I would like to be a Carlisle man."

So it was that in early February of 1904 I found myself on a train again. This time, though, it was the Frisco Railroad and I was taking the long journey east to Pennsylvania. My decision had pleased Pa no end. My going off to Carlisle was a dream come true to him. Even before that recruiter came our way, Pa had been in contact with our Indian agent about the possibility of me going to one of the big Indian schools on the East Coast, either Hampton Institute or Carlisle. I found out years later what he'd said to the agent.

"I want my boy to go and make something of himself, for he cannot do it here."

Despite our struggles, Pa always wanted the best for me. Maybe we butted heads so much because we were so similar. I was the only one who ever stood up to him. Hiram P. Thorpe could scare anyone in the county. Even his brothers gave him a wide berth. But he could never control me. And as much as that frustrated him, I think it also gratified him that his boy had such grit. He believed in me, and that was why, even though Pa was not a man much given to smiles, there was a big grin on his face when he nodded goodbye to me as the train pulled out.

It was the longest journey I'd ever taken. I had time to think as that train rolled on. I watched out the window as we passed over the plains where the buffalo herds our people had hunted no longer roamed, through snow-covered fields now owned by white farmers, over rivers where no Indian canoes floated, on into states where the lights of the towns made it hard to see the night stars. As we rattled past little whistle-stops and rumbled through big cities, what I mostly thought about were the last words Pa spoke to me before I got on board.

"Son," he said, "you are an Indian. I want you to show other races what an Indian can do."

FOLLOW THE TROLLEY TRACKS

It was February 6, 1904, when I first set foot in Carlisle, Pennsylvania. But from where I stood on the train platform I saw no sign of the Carlisle Indian Industrial School. The sun was shining and I suppose it was a warm winter day by Pennsylvania standards. But I felt cold to the bone as the wind whistled around me. Plus I was confused as I stood there holding the cloth valise that held what few clothes I owned. Which way was I supposed to go?

I'd been too shy to talk to anyone on the train. There hadn't been any other Indians on board and the white people pretty much ignored me in my silence. Some might not have even recognized me as an Indian. My skin, though browned by the sun, was never as dark as Pa's or Ma's and I was the one child in the family who'd inherited the Irish jaw of Pa's white father. My light skin and my features had gotten me into more than one scuffle when I'd first arrived at Haskell. Some of the Indian kids from other tribes had called me "Half-breed" or even "White Boy." But nobody ever called me those names more than once. Those were fighting words and even when I lost a tussle, the one I went up against ended up at least as bruised and bloody as me.

I sighed at that memory. I knew what was likely coming at Carlisle. Once again, before they discovered how tough a Thorpe can be, I'd be hearing those names aimed at me like poison-tipped arrows. First, though, before I could be insulted, I'd have to find the danged place.

I tried to remember the scant intructions the recruiter had given me.

"You can't miss the school," he'd said. "It is directly to the northeast of the town square."

What town square? Again I sighed. I hated to do it, but I would have to ask someone. A dark-skinned man in a uniform and a red cap was leaning against a wall. I knew from his uniform that he was a porter. Because I didn't have any luggage, he was making a point of not noticing me. I went over to him.

"Excuse me, sir," I said. "Can I ask you a question?"

For some reason, that not only got his attention but brought a little smile to his face.

"Sir? Is that what you said?" he asked me.

"Yes sir," I answered. "I'm looking for the U.S. Indian School."

The man nodded at that. "I see. Well, I am happy to help a young gentleman like yourself. You just follow those trolley tracks. They will lead you to the entrance. Right up Garrison Street there. Can you read that sign?"

"Thank you, sir," I said. "I appreciate your help."

"No, young man, thank you," he replied, patting

my arm with his hand. "This is the nicest conversation I've had all day."

Valise in hand, I trudged along those trolley tracks toward what had been the Carlisle Military Barracks before it became the first great Indian boarding school twenty-five years before my arrival. I probably ought to tell you something about the history of the place. Not that I knew all of this on that day when I arrived, as green as a cornstalk in May.

Major Richard Henry Pratt was the force behind not just Carlisle but the whole idea of Indian boarding schools. After fighting in the Civil War, he had been sent west in 1867 to serve at Fort Sill in Indian Territory. His job was to keep the tribes on their reservations and protect the white settlers, but he soon found that he liked the Indians and got along with them. He even admired them for their honesty and their intelligence. His next job was to take a group of Cheyenne Indian warriors off to Fort Marion in Florida in 1875. But instead of treating those Indian prisoners of war as hostiles, he decided to take another approach. He dressed them in army uniforms and treated them like military recruits. Rather than fighting them, he wanted to educate them to be just like white men, speak English, hold down jobs, and give up their old ways.

There was a lot of liberal people in the East who agreed with his ideas that an Indian was just a white man bathed in red. They liked his motto: Kill the Indian and save the man. The government liked his ideas, too. Fighting the Indian was costing more money than it would to civilize him. I think part of it, too, was because they figured that having the children of powerful Indian leaders sent off to school would help keep the tribes in line. With their sons and daughters held as hostages in faraway Pennsylvania, they'd be more likely to do as they was told.

So it was that the abandoned military barracks at Carlisle opened up in 1879 as the first big Indian boarding school, with Major Pratt (who was promoted to captain and then colonel) at the head of it. It quickly became a model school.

As I walked along I saw a six-foot-tall picket fence ahead of me. That was the fence that surrounded the whole school. There was a big wooden gate at the entrance. I stopped, though, before I got there. There was a store alongside the road. FLICKINGERS read the sign. Displayed in its window were souvenirs for the tourists who came in droves to Carlisle. Wagonloads would come in the fall to the football games on Indian Field, and even in the summer, about three hundred people every day would visit to gawk at the uniformed Indian youths.

On this February morning, though, there weren't any tourists in sight. The few folks in the store were not paying any mind to the things I found myself staring at in that front window. In front were rows of postcards with before and after photos of Carlisle students, showing them as they arrived with their long hair and buckskin clothing and regalia and then

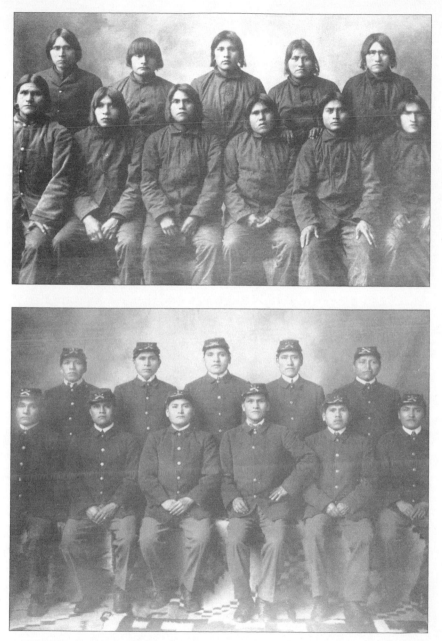

Before and after photos of Carlisle students (from 1907), including Louis Tewanima (bottom row, second from left in the before photo; top row, first from left in the after photo)

what they looked like after they'd had their hair cut and had been dressed in school uniforms. I'm sure those pictures were what drew most folks' attention, but what I liked best were the little triangle-shaped flags, bright pennants of crimson and gold. CARLISLE was written across the face of each of them. I decided right then and there that I would get me one of those pennants the first chance I had.

But not right now. I turned away from the window and started walking again. There was a differerent world waiting for me on the other side of that picket fence. I was excited and more than a little uncertain. But I was careful not to show any of that on my face as I passed through the big wooden gate to start my new life.

CADET THORPE

At first glance, the Carlisle Indian school was pretty to behold. Its big wooden buildings were painted white, and elm trees rose up around them like fountains. The twenty or so acres of the school was set up on a knoll and I could see how clean it was all kept. The lawns laid out around the walkways were just as neat as a pin.

I wasn't quite sure where I should head off to, seeing as how no one was there to pay any attention to me. On that day in February when I arrived, the student population of Carlisle stood at 598 boys (which with my addition would now be 599) and 470 girls. Of course, just as it had been at Haskell, although they called us boys and girls, the Carlisle students ranged in age from little children to men and women in their thirties. But at the moment there was not a soul to be seen. I guessed they were all inside at classes. So, after studying the lay of the land a bit, I went over to the nearest building. A tall, white-haired white woman saw me approaching and came outside.

"Are you a new student?" she asked, taking note of my valise.

"Yes, ma'am," I answered.

"Well," she said, "you are not headed here. These

are the girls' quarters. You shall want the large boys' quarters. Do you know anyone here at Carlisle?"

"Yes, ma'am," I said, holding out my papers from our Indian agent.

"Oh," she said, brightening a bit as she read them. "Sac and Fox. I believe there are about eight boys and girls from your tribe here already. Our Emma Newashe is one of your people."

"Yes, ma'am," I said, continuing to hold up my end of the conversation.

"Her brother Bill is in the large boys' quarters. He is an excellent baseball player and quite a good addition to the lineup. He and his sister are both fine, upstanding examples. They have learned how to stick to it."

"I'm glad to hear that, ma'am," I said, finally having a chance to prove that my vocabulary consisted of more than two words.

She handed the papers back to me. "Take these to the guardhouse." She held out her arm to point a long finger down one of the walks. "That is where you must report in as a new student."

"Thank you, ma'am," I said.

"You are welcome, young man. Remember, you shall do well here if you stick to it."

That was one of Colonel Pratt's mottos, I soon learned.

I stuck to the path, and found the guardhouse without any trouble. It turned out that I would not have much trouble finding that guardhouse a few more times while at Carlisle. It was where students were sent when they broke one too many rules. This time, though, they didn't find a cell for me there. The officer just checked my papers and sent me on down another path, this one paved with wooden slats, to the school hospital.

"Strip and wash," I was told next. I'd had enough experience with Indian schools to know that this was standard procedure for any new student. They looked me over like they were examining a horse before deciding to trade for it, then pronounced me sound enough to serve.

I handed in the boots and jeans and shirt and coat and underthings I'd been wearing, all folded into a neat bundle. They also took my valise, which just held more of the same.

"No jewelry? Rings, bracelets, necklaces, or the like?" asked the clerk who took my belongings. His voice and the look on his face showed his disappointment. The beautiful clothing and fine jewelry that most Carlisle students were sent off with by their families—wanting their young ones to make a good impression—always ended up being sold by the administrators at Carlisle, with none of the profits ever going to the students who lost their finery.

In my case, you might say I got the better of the trade. For my rancher's go-to-town clothes, I got back a set of red flannel long johns, two nightshirts, underwear, new shoes, a black suit, a uniform, and a hat to top it all off. I was also issued bedding and towels and a trunk to stow everything.

There was just enough time before assembly for me to make my way to the large boys' quarters. I put my trunk by the bed in a room I'd be sharing with two other boys. The bugle sounded and I hustled out to take my position outside the dormitory and stand at attention with all the other Indian boys wearing the same uniform as mine. I was now Cadet Thorpe of Carlisle.

THE ROUTINE

Routine. That was the ticket at Carlisle. The school was run tighter than a military post. Having been at Haskell, I thought I knew what routine was like, but Haskell couldn't hold a candle to Carlisle. "Keep them moving" was the way Colonel Pratt put it. That way, or so his theory went, there'd be no time for homesickness or mischief or regret. I guess what he didn't take into account was the fact that you might still be feeling all three of those, even when you were marching in uniform.

We got up at 5:30 A.M., made our beds, washed, dressed, lined up, and marched to breakfast at 6:15. Breakfast, like every other meal, was itself a military affair. Your table manners were watched over by a student monitor, quick to tell you what to do with your napkin and how to properly hold a knife and a fork. We were waited on by female Carlisle students, and that was as close as we were allowed to get to them at any time. They kept the boys and girls strictly separate during every other part of the day, and although we were allowed to say a polite thank-you when we were served pancakes or potatoes or whatever, we were not to make eye contact.

There were lots of ways you could break the rules at

Carlisle, including a lack of neatness in your uniform or failing to obey orders quick enough and the like. But—aside from doing something that was "acting savage," such as talking in your Native language—it seemed as if the strictest penalties were given to anyone who even seemed to be thinking about what they called lewd behavior. There was no socializing in the common areas, no visiting of the dormitories.

Jim, right, with two other Carlisle students, 1904

Keeping the boys and girls apart even extended into the weekends. Saturdays, Carlisle students were allowed to ride the trolley down into town, but it was set up so that boys went one Saturday and girls went the next. Sundays, we were all expected to go to religious services, but we were kept separate there, too. When the students marched off campus to the church of their choice, the boys all had to march down one street while the girls marched down another.

Fraternizing with the opposite sex in any way—talking, passing a note, even smiling at each other—was watched out for by our company officers, who were Carlisle students themselves. If you were caught, you'd be sent off to the court, which was also run by students, where you could expect both to be found guilty and to be punished with loss of privileges or confinement or hard labor, depending on how bad your offense was.

The joke around campus, or so my roommate George told me, was that if a cadet was ever caught actually holding hands with a girl he would be shot by a firing squad. That was funny, but not that funny. Everyone learned quick that when you were at Carlisle there was a right way and a wrong way to behave in just about every aspect of your life and that the final word on what was good or bad always came down right from the top, from Pratt himself.

George, who was Sioux, had a great Indian sense of humor. I wish I'd been able to spend more time with him. We got to be friends pretty quick, even though he was the first one to get into a tussle with me.

"What's your Indian name?" he said the first night I was at Carlisle. "Buttermilk?"

By that he was referring to the color of my skin, of course. After we had wrestled around a bit and I had him down with his face on the floor and his arm on his back, he changed his tune.

"All right," he grunted. "So maybe I just call you Jim."

But even though I'd beat him in wrestling, George still kept that teasing up, though in a friendly way. That was one of the things that made me like him so much.

During our precious little bit of free time, George and I would often amuse ourselves playing shinny—which is our old Indian game of field hockey—on the playground next to the guardhouse. I was better with my stick than any of the others. In our first game I had scored four goals before the other side had even threatened us.

"Better watch out, Jim," George said. "Pop Warner is going to take notice of you and make you one of his boys. The way you run, he put you on his track team and wear you out."

That got a smile from me. Being chosen as one of Pop's boys was far from a threat. It was one of the greatest privileges at Carlisle. Glenn S. Warner, who had been known as "Pop," since he had been a slightly overage football star himself, was the coach of the track and football teams at Carlisle. Both teams hardly ever lost, and sports at Carlisle had become even more famous under his stern hand.

Pop Warner was already a legend by 1904. He was known for inventing all kinds of new trick plays and formations. He was the first one to ever tell players on the line to get down into something like a sprinter's stance and not just stand with their hands on their knees at the start of a play. In fact, though it hadn't yet happened by the time I got to Carlisle, one of the first forward passes in the history of the game would be thrown by Frank Mt. Pleasant, one of Pop's Indian quarterbacks. Pop Warner had coached at other famous schools before Carlisle, but it was here that he had done—and would do— the most.

But I never got to work with Pop Warner that year. He took little notice of an Indian boy too small and slight to be any good on the gridiron. Maybe if he had seen me run or play baseball, things would have been different. Maybe if things had gone different in my own life I would have become one of Pop Warner's boys that year.

But maybe not. Even though none of us knew it at the time, big changes were in the wind at Carlisle Industrial School. Colonel Pratt was at war with his own superiors in the War Department. Later on that same year, Colonel Pratt would leave the school.

At the time, though, I took little note of any of that. Other things were on my mind. Just as I was getting settled in to Carlisle, I got another one of those messages from home that I had come to dread. It was hard for me to believe, but the emptiness I felt in my heart told me that it was true. On April 24, 1904, at the young age of fifty-two, Hiram P. Thorpe passed away from blood poisoning. My pa was dead.

OUTING

I can't remember much of the rest of that spring. I felt like an ox that had been hit with a poleax. I could have gotten permission to make a visit back home if I'd wanted, but there was no point to it. By the time the message reached me, the funeral was long over and my pa was in the ground.

And now who was there for me to go home to with both Ma and Pa dead? Sure, there were my brothers and sisters. But they were no longer at home. They had all been farmed out like me to Indian schools in Oklahoma and Kansas. The only ones still left in our cabin were my stepma, who was expecting again, and the two little children she and Pa had before he passed. Even if I wanted to go there, I knew there would be no room for me.

So, for lack of anywhere else in the world to go, I stayed at Carlisle. I got up and went to bed with the bugle, marched to meals and classes with the other cadets like I had done before. I went to my assignment in the tailor shop. It wasn't electrical engineering—which was not offered at Carlisle, despite what that recruiter led me to believe. I suppose I learned a good bit about the tailoring trade, but my heart wasn't in much of anything. At times I felt as if I was somewhere else, just watching my hands work from a distance, observing my body get dressed and march and eat and sleep, but not being a part of it. I was drifting like a feather caught in the current of a slow river.

It was getting close to summer. The other students, some of them with a good bit of eagerness, were talking about going off on the Outing program. Not only was it a way for them to get away from the military routine at Carlisle, but they'd have a chance to earn some real cash money.

I guess I should explain what the Outing program was. It was one of Colonel Pratt's favorite programs that he invented. What it meant was that during the three months of summer, and sometimes for even longer, a good percentage of our Carlisle boys and girls would be sent off to work on farms. The idea was that it would teach Indian students about life in the outside world and prepare them for their eventual careers as menial workers.

Half the money that you earned was sent straight back to Carlisle, where it was put into an interest-bearing account in your name. The other half you were given in cash. It was never that much, considering that the average Outing wages were only about $6.50 a month plus room and board. The average wage for workers who did what we did back then was more than twice that much. So our $6.50 a month was equal to less than half of what was minimum wage back then. (Those farmers got a real bargain!)

The thought of going out to earn money didn't really excite me. I figured I didn't have to worry about money. Arrangements had been made back in Oklahoma to provide a guardian to look after my interests. When the land deal was done with the Sac and Foxes, every enrolled member of the tribe, myself included, had been given an annuity. Mine was close to $50 a year. I also inherited my part of the rent paid by the ranchers who were working the lands that had been part of Ma and Pa's allotments. I was not wealthy by any means, but when you added up the annuities and the rent, I guessed I'd be getting at least $150 a year.

However, every Carlisle student had to take part in Outing at one time or another. You didn't have a choice. So it was that on June 17, 1904, I was sent off to Summerdale, Pennsylvania, to the farm of Mr. A. E. Buckholz. It was a nice enough place, there on the Susquehanna River. The river, in fact, was the best part of it. My first thought was that it would be fun to fish there. But there was no time for fishing—or even getting outdoors at all—as far as old A.E. was concerned.

Superintendent Pratt's idea of an ideal Outing experience was that it would bring an Indian boy or girl into a white home almost as part of the family. They would be a gentle and civilizing influence on you. You'd learn English by talking it every day and you'd eat your meals with the family and, when you weren't working, you'd spend time with them.

But old A.E. was as stern and unpleasant a man as you could imagine. If he had ever smiled it probably would have cracked his face. His wife and his children were just as sour as he was. It was as if they were all sucking pickles from the way they looked all the time. It was a good thing I knew English before I got to Mr. A. E. Buckholz's place, because the only words I would have learned from him were "Wake up" and "Get back to work."

Healthy outside work was what Superintendent Pratt expected us to do on farms. I wouldn't much have minded that. But the only time I saw the outside was when I was either told to bring in wood or allowed to go to the outhouse. I was kept in the kitchen sixteen hours a day, scrubbing, mopping, cleaning, peeling potatoes. I even had to eat my meals in the kitchen. All that for a generous $6.50 a month.

Stick to it might have been the Carlisle model, but what I had to endure stuck in my craw. After a month of being old A.E.'s scullery boy, I'd had enough of his civilizing influence. I took off.

Running off, as you know, was no new thing for me. But this time it was different. There was no home for me to run to. So where I ran was not away but back. Even though I knew I would end up spending at least a few days in the guardhouse, where I ran was back to Carlisle.

Running away was nothing unusual for a Carlisle student to do. Boys and girls ran away from the school all the time. In fact, during all the years it existed, more students ran away from the Carlisle Indian Industrial School than ever earned a certificate from it. The only thing different about what I did—and that may be why my stay in the guardhouse turned out to only be a few days—was that I ran *back* to school rather than away from it.

So, instead of trying to send me right out again, they let me go to summer classes. I was assigned back to the tailor shop and began spending time with my friends. I started laughing at George's jokes again. Somehow, the experience of being sent off to that awful farm, bad as it was, had been good for me. I no longer felt like I was walking around with the clouds around my head.

I also started taking part in sports. I wasn't on any of the school teams, but there were intramural sports going on all the time at Carlisle for the smaller boys and girls or those who didn't have the athletic talent to go into competition against other schools. What we played was one shop against another, with the tailors versus the blacksmiths or the harness shop and so on. I became the starting pitcher on the baseball squad and also earned a spot as a guard when the tailors played football. We didn't have much real equipment, but we made do with whatever we had and our football games looked like the real thing.

It wasn't that hard to do in those days. Football then was a lot different than it would be in only a few years. For example, the idea of wearing any kind of headgear was just starting to come into the game.

And when we lined up against another team, there was no neutral area in between. Also, just about anybody, including a guard like me, could be the ballcarrier. Slugging, tripping, everything short of eye gouging and biting might go on when you were in the middle of a flying wedge trying to force your way through the other team. I loved it.

Although big changes had not yet come to the game of football in that year of 1904, they surely did come to the U.S. Indian School at Carlisle. Superintendent Pratt had been at odds with the Indian Department for some time. It was mostly because of his beliefs, which were that Indians were just as good as any other person. Yes, he wanted us to give up our languages and our customs and be just like white people. But he believed that once an Indian did that, he or she could be just as successful as any white man. In his estimation, Indians were just as smart as anyone. Total assimilation of all the Indians into the United States was his goal. That belief of his was why his supporters called him the "Red Man's Moses."

About the time I was sent off on that first Outing program, things came to a head. The War Department relieved Colonel Pratt of his duties at Carlisle and appointed Captain William A. Mercer as the new superintendent of the school.

Captain Mercer liked sports just as much as Colonel Pratt. If anything, he liked them even better. The biggest changes brought by our new superintendent had nothing to do with athletics. They had to do with what our new leader felt Indians were capable of.

I don't want to bore you with too much talk about what we had to study. To say it as simple as possible, Colonel Pratt made sure that on top of our vocational training, we also studied what they now call the liberal arts. Not only were we expected to learn history and government, biology, and mathematics, we also had to take courses in art, where we were taught how to paint still lifes. We read Shakespeare and put on plays. Students wrote poems.

Once Captain Mercer arrived, things got much more practical at Carlisle. All of us saw right away that things were different. Those classroom courses weren't cut out, but they were put to the side. What was in favor now was more vocational training and military drills. Poems and paintings were now nowhere near as important as marching and learning how to work with our hands. I know that bothered some of the students.

On the positive side of things, though, some of the social rules were relaxed. Everyone liked that. Now it was actually possible for boys and girls to talk to one another and mingle some—with chaperones present. We was even allowed to have dances two or three times a week.

That year went pretty fast for me. In what seemed no time at all it was 1905. One of the things that hadn't changed was the Outing program. It fit right in with Superintendent Mercer's idea about making Indians into good workers. So I was sent off again in March to work on the farm owned by Mr. James L. Cadwallader in Doolington, Pennsylvania. This time, it really was farmwork that I was expected to do. Being outside with cows and pigs, working the fields to put the spring crops in and all, I felt as if I was back home, even if those thick green fields and that dark soil was so different from back in Oklahoma Territory. The Cadwallader boys took me fishing with them and I showed them how to make snares to catch rabbits and raccoons. Instead of being banished to the kitchen, I ate my meals at the dinner table with the family and was treated polite like a human being. My three months there was not bad at all and I was feeling good when I returned to the U.S. Indian School in July. For me, at least, the Carlisle way of education was working out okay.

As a matter of fact, my counselors decided that Outing had been so good for me that as soon as I got back to Carlisle they sent me right out again, this time to a farm in Robbinsville, New Jersey. I did so well there over the next year and a half that I ended up being promoted to be a foreman. By the time I got back to Carlisle in March of 1907, I'd spent fourteen months at school and twenty-two months away as a laborer.

Much as I had enjoyed the outside work, I missed my friends at Carlisle. I missed the excitement of marching to the sound of the school band and taking part in close-order drilling and wearing a uniform. And I also missed sports. I still had the dream of playing something more than just intramural. Now that I was bigger and stronger, I believed I was good enough to become a varsity player.

But wouldn't you know it? Just as soon as I got back to Carlisle, they sent me right back out again to a farm near Trenton. I wasn't happy about that. I was ready to do something else with my life. Another baseball season was starting and I would not be a part of it.

After being in Trenton for three weeks I figured I'd had enough of the Outing program. One morning I just picked up my bag and walked. I kept on walking till I got to the trolley station. Back in those days, you could get most anywhere by trolley for only a few cents. I rode it to the end of its line at the edge of town, walked a ways, and hopped onto the trolley that led through the next town. I was back in Carlisle by the end of the following day.

Of course I knew what was waiting for me. I went straight to the the dank old guardhouse and gave them a salute.

"Cadet Thorpe, Runaway First Class, reporting for imprisonment," I said.

That got a chuckle out of them, but it still didn't get me out of having to spend enough time in the guardhouse to get pretty familiar with every one of the stones inside my cell. I had plenty of time for thinking. None of it was about accepting another Outing assignment. One way or another, my life was going to take a different path from here on in.

CLEARING THE BAR

It was now April of 1907. I was nineteen years old. Daffodils were in bloom along the walkways, the little birds had returned to their nests, and I was back playing pickup football games with my friends. I've generally been pretty good at most games, but what I've always loved best is anything that has a ball in it, baseball and football in particular. I didn't really have any plans to be a track star.

It was late in the day. My friend Billy Newashe and I were walking across the upper track field on our way to a pickup football game with one of our scrub teams.

Bill pointed with his chin toward a group of upper-classmen in tracksuits gathered around one end of the field.

"What are they up to?" he said.

As we got closer, it became pretty plain to me. They were gathered around the jumping pit. They paid no attention to us. They were members of the varsity track team, Pop Warner's boys. We were just scrubs. They were doing the high jump. They kept going higher and higher. Finally, they set the bar at five feet nine inches—about as high as the top of my head. None of them was able to clear that height.

"It's more like what they're *not* up to," I joked. That got a smile out of Bill.

Right after I spoke, one of those bigger boys turned to his friends.

"We're done for the day," he said. "No one's gonna clear the bar at that height."

"Can I take a try at it?" I asked, stepping forward

They all turned and looked at me like I was a worm. I had a pair of overalls on, a hickory shirt, and a pair of gymnasium shoes I had picked up that belonged to someone else. I looked like anything but a high jumper.

"Go ahead," I was told. I know they figured I would fall on my you-know-what. They snickered as I took a couple of short runs and kicked a few times to limber up. But their snickering stopped dead when I sailed over the bar. I was the one who was laughing when Bill and I left to go down to the lower field for our game. Those track boys just stood there with their mouths open, looking at the bar I'd cleared on my first try.

The next day I was in class when a message was brought in to my teacher. She read it and then looked hard at me.

Oh-oh, I thought. Was I in trouble?

"James Thorpe," she said, "you are to report to the office of Coach Warner at the end of class."

I have to admit that I was in awe of Coach Warner. No man ever did more to change football into the game it is today. I know I've already said that, but maybe this little list of some of his innovations will give you an idea of just how important he was to the game. He invented the screen play, the single- and double-wing formations, the reverse, the three-point stance, the spiral punt, the use of shoulder and thigh pads, and putting numbers on players' jerseys.

By 1907 football had become a game where a coach who knew how to think could lead even a medio-cre team to victory. A first down was now ten yards, instead of the original five. Seven men had to be on the line of scrimmage. That opened up the field of play and made brute force plays like the flying wedge a thing of the past. Hitting someone in the face was now illegal. They'd added more officials to make sure those rules were followed. Four officials were now on the field for every game. They had also made it legal to throw a forward pass of more than ten yards. However, passing rules were different from what they would be later. If a pass was not caught on first down or second down, you got a fifteen-yard penalty. An incomplete pass on third down was ruled a turnover, as was any pass that hit the ground without being touched by one of your players.

How did I know all that? I'd been making it a point to learn everything I could about those new football rules since coming back to school. I wrote them down in the back of one of my notebooks.

But until that day I was called to his office, I'd never met Pop Warner, who, in addition to being the football coach, was also the track coach. I knew how fiercely he defended his athletes and everything to do with his sports program. I had a feeling that I knew why I was being called to his office. He was going to give me holy heck for interfering with his athletic boys practicing their high-jumping. Somebody had probably seen me laughing at them. For all I knew, I might be on my way back to the guardhouse.

I knocked on his office door.

"Come on in," a deep voice growled.

Pop Warner looked up at me from behind his desk as I came on in.

"You wanted to see me, Coach?"

He looked me up and down. "Are those the clothes you had on yesterday when you made the high jump?" he asked.

I nodded my head, figuring I was in for it now.

"Do you know what you've done?"

"Nothing bad, I hope," I said.

"Bad?" Pop Warner's blocky face opened into a grin. "Boy, you've just broken a school record. That bar was set at five nine."

"That's not very high," I said. "I think I could do better in a tracksuit." I wasn't bragging, just stating the honest truth.

Pop Warner stood up and put an arm around my shoulder. "Well, you go on down to the clubhouse and exchange those overalls. You're on my track team now."

KEEP A-GOIN'

April 26 was Arbor Day. I'd been looking forward to it for weeks. Each of our classrooms planted a tree on that day. Our class, Mr. Henderson's room 9, put in an elm tree along the road to the greenhouse.

But that wasn't what I was most excited about. Arbor Day was also a big sports day, the day of the school intramural track meet.

Mr. Henderson rubbed his hands together as he looked at our little squad, led by Ed Twohearts, Walter Hunt, and me.

"Boys," he said, "we are going to show them what for."

Sure enough, that was what we did. Our sixth-grade class beat out all the upper classes. I won the 120-yard hurdles and the high jump and finished second in the 220-yard dash. Walter and Ed did just about as well and caught Pop Warner's eye. He added them onto Carlisle's track team along with me.

There's one more student athlete I ought to mention who made a good showing that Arbor Day. His being a member of the varsity track team was as unlikely as the way he ended up at Carlisle. The U.S. government had been having trouble with the Hopis, an Indian tribe out in Arizona. Those Hopis weren't making war, like the Sioux. They were just plain refusing to do what they were told when it came to sending their young people to the new Indian school that had been built out at a place called Moqui near the Hopi Reservation.

Our fathers warned us to have nothing to do with the ways of the whites, they said. *We were warned not to let our children go to your school.*

Even after the government arrested a bunch of Hopi leaders and sent them off to Alcatraz prison, they still kept on defying that order to send their children to school. It ended up with President Roosevelt sending in troops. The two main Hopi leaders were banished for life from their reservation. Seventy-two others were sent off to do roadwork, and a bunch of Hopi men were imprisoned at an army fort. Another seventeen young Hopi men were sent off to Carlisle. They were as much hostages as they were students. They had to serve a five-year sentence at Carlisle.

Right about the time I was getting out of the guardhouse, those Hopis were making the acquaintance of Pop Warner. Their leader was Louis Tewanima. He was thirty years old, even though he looked to be about half that age and was so small that he was knee-high to a gopher. When they arrived at Carlisle on January 26, 1907, he and the other Hopis had been examined by the school doctor before being sent off to their dormitory.

That was the usual practice at Carlisle by then, making sure they had not brought anything in the way of lice or sickness. Of course the doctor never mentioned the fact that lots of Carlisle students only got sick *after* they came to the school. The school graveyard, a place I didn't like to even think about, was full of far too many graves of young men and women who never saw their homes and families again.

What the school doctor noted about Louis Tewanima was that he was undernourished and in poor physical condition. He had round shoulders, a prominent clavicle (which meant his chest bone stuck out like a chicken's), and an emaciated look.

Just like every other wild Indian who was sent to Carlisle, the Hopis had their clothes taken away and their hair cut off. The one thing that wasn't taken from them was their earrings. I guess they made it clear that you'd have to cut their ears off to get them. Seeing as how they couldn't seem to speak a word of English, those twelve Hopi "boys" were put into a special class. Every day was spent drilling English into them.

Even though they could hardly speak English, they somehow got the word that there was running going on. Whenever they had free time they went over to the track and watched. Pop Warner took notice of them, but was unimpressed. All he saw was a wild bunch of scrawny, undersized Indians with huge earrings and furtive eyes.

"We want to suit up," Louis said one day, making a gesture with his hands to indicate himself and the others.

Pop Warner looked down at him in surprise. "What for? You're not big enough for anything."

"We Hopis run fast good," Louis said in a voice that was quiet but self-confident. "All Hopis run fast good."

Pop Warner shrugged. "Go ahead," he said. He figured it wouldn't hurt to let them try. After a while they'd just tire themselves out and realize track was not for them.

But as soon as they had those uniforms on, the twelve Hopis began to run. They circled the track once, twice, and kept on going. Five minutes passed and they were still running. Fifteen minutes, half an hour, and they had not slowed their pace one bit. That was when Pop Warner realized what he had. Louis Tewanima and those other Hopis were some of the best long-distance runners in the world.

You may not know much about Hopis, which was the case with Pop Warner before he met Louis Tewanima, but they just about live to run. Back home in his village of Shongopavi up on Second Mesa, Louis had been running since he was a little spindle-legged boy. Just like I'd done in Oklahoma Territory, he had chased down jackrabbits barefoot. There were also races that they would run from time to time, kicking a ball or a stick for twenty miles or so. In fact, running was so much a part of his life that Louis and his friends hadn't thought anything of running all the way to Winslow, Arizona, and back just to watch the trains go by. That was a 120-mile round-trip!

Everybody at school had heard about what good runners Louis and the others were by the time Arbor Day came around. We all watched them. Their teacher lined them up in front of the little oak tree they'd planted.

"Ready?" she said, holding up both hands. Then, although their pronunciation was a little off, they sang the first two verses of "America the Beautiful." That wasn't all, though. They also sang, with considerably more effort, the school fight song. That song had been written by none other than Pop Warner himself.

You play another team today.
Keep a-goin'.
You've been playing pretty well,
No don't take a breathing spell,
Give the stands a chance to yell,
Keep a-goin'.

If you strike a tougher bunch
Keep a-goin'.
You only need a harder punch,
Keep a-goin'.

Tain't no use to stand and whine
When they're coming through the line,
Hitch your trousers up and climb
Keep a-goin'.

Later on that day, in the long-distance races, that was just what Louis Tewanima did. He was an easy winner, going just as fast at the end when he crossed the line as he'd been running at the start. He nodded to me when they gave him his ribbon and I nodded back.

Keep a-goin', I thought. That's the ticket.

That was how Louis did it and, by golly, I was going to do the same. I knew in my heart that kind of determination would take us somewhere.

EX

That spring of 1907 I played my part, but I wasn't the star of the Carlisle track team. Still, as one of Pop Warner's boys, I was looked at as a hero. I liked the attention, though I tried not to show how proud it made me feel. That's the old Sac and Fox way. The people who are most admired are those who don't spend their time admiring themselves. Pa always used to tell me how our great chief Black Hawk was the most modest man of all in his time.

In fact, I don't think I changed the way I acted any at all. I had new friends—the other boys on the team—but I still kept my same old friends and spent time with them whenever I could.

Those new friends were great people, some of whom I'd hardly dared to say a word to before. The best man on our team was Frank Mt. Pleasant, a Tuscarora from western New York State. Frank was almost as quiet as I was and he sure didn't look that big or that athletic. In fact, I learned later that when he first arrived at Carlisle, he'd been marked by the doctor as having a weak heart. That heart of Frank Mt. Pleasant's turned out to be a lot stronger than anyone expected. At just about every track meet Carlisle went to, he would win the 100, the 220, and the broad jump. In 1908, he ended up being one of the first two Carlisle athletes to be sent to the Olympic Games.

I always liked the idea of doing more than one event in track, and I guess you could say that Frank inspired me to keep thinking that way. Of course, our Carlisle team was always so much smaller than any other school's that our athletes had to compete in multiple events. Sometimes that meant running just as fast from one event to the other as we did when we were actually doing the events themselves.

Frank was also the quarterback for the Carlisle football team. And he was a great one. You could say, in fact, that Frank Mt. Pleasant was the first quarterback to really perfect the forward pass. Football and track, I thought. If Frank Mt. Pleasant can do it, so can I.

Most of Frank's encouragement to me was in the way of a nod now and then when I did well in the 120 hurdles or the high jump. Those were the two events Coach Warner assigned me to at first. What he planned for me that spring was to "get some seasoning," as he put it.

"We're just going to let you get your feet wet," he said. "Do well enough and we'll really throw you in the deep water next season."

I was pretty sure that Pop Warner expected some big things of me. Albert Exendine was an indication of that. Ex, as everybody always called him, had been a great track man, especially in the high jump and shot put. He had also been one of the best players on

74

Pop's football team, a tough-nosed tackle. He and Pop had always got on real well together. So it was probably no surprise to anyone that in the spring of 1907, Pop invited Ex, who had already graduated, to come back to Carlisle as a coach. Ex was getting ready to attend law school at Dickinson. Being able to live at Carlisle while he was doing that would help both him and Pop Warner's teams. Plus Ex loved to be kept physically active.

What was a surprise—to me at least—was that Pop Warner handed me over to his old friend and former player as a special project. Boy, did I love that! Not only was Ex the kind of athlete I wanted to be, he was also an Oklahoma boy. His dad was Cherokee and his mom was Delaware, and he had grown up around Bartlesville and Anadarko. Another Okie Indian! That meant we had a lot in common, including the same kind of sense of humor. We did a lot of teasing after we had gotten to know each other.

I was still working in the tailor shop, so that was one way Ex could gently needle me.

"When are you going to make me a suit?" he would say.

"Soon as you make me a cake," I'd crack back. That was because Ex had always been assigned to the bakery at Carlisle.

"At least I always been smart enough to stay close to the food," he'd reply.

"Oh, I can see that for sure," I'd say, looking at his stomach.

Sometimes it would end up with the two of us wrestling around. I only weighed 155 pounds. Even though he had about 50 pounds on me, it was a pretty even match and we'd usually both end up on the ground, laughing.

We also made our share of jokes about Carlisle itself.

For example, now that I was one of Pop's boys, I got to eat at the special training table. "The food is just as bad here as it was at my old table," I might say.

"It surely is," Ex would reply, "and the best part is that there's more of it!"

Or when it came summer and most of the other students were heading off to be cheap labor for some farmer, Ex would nod to me and say, "Well, young Thorpe, there goes your chance to be independently wealthy."

"Yes," I'd say, pretending to wipe a tear from my eye, "I surely am going to miss those beautiful potato fields."

That was because Pop Warner's boys never got sent off in the Outing program. Our summer jobs were to train and keep on training. I had ended up doing well enough that first season at track to win my first varsity letter, a big red *C* that I had sewed onto my shirt. I hadn't won any events, but with the help of Ex's coaching I'd taken a second in the high jump against the University of Pennsylvania and two more seconds in the high hurdles and the high jump against Bucknell. I was on my way!

15

SUMMER AT CARLISLE

Summer of 1907 at Carlisle. That was a good one for me. We still had to get up early, follow a schedule, and respond to the bells and formations, but it was a far cry from laboring in some farmer's fields, hoeing endless rows under the hot sun. Not only that, with so many fewer people at the school, life took on a whole different tempo. Only about two hundred of us Indian students remained at Carlisle, while the other eight hundred or so were off scattered all around the northeast.

Of course, not everyone who was off campus was working on farms. Some of them were off doing far more interesting things. There was our school band, for example. Every one of those boys was just as good as any professional musician and they had a regular engagement every summer working at a big resort on the New Jersey shore. Some of them managed to salt away some decent tips.

Then there was the baseball players. It was the practice for the varsity nine and a good many of our football players—most of whom were good at baseball, too—to make some money every summer playing ball. They scattered around the northeast and even farther to various semipro and minor-league teams.

Charlie Roy, captain of the varsity nine in 1907, went off to Newark. Joe Twin was playing in the Williams Valley League. Bill Newashe and Pete Hauser, both of whom were football starters, had been hired on by Hagerstown, Maryland, while our left end, Bill Gardner, was playing for Sunbury.

Of course it wasn't just Indian college students who did that. It was pretty common practice in those days for college boys to spend their summer making a few dollars playing in the minors and then come back to their school teams in the fall. Earning money from summer baseball was something I knew I would be able to do in the future. I looked forward to that.

Playing summer ball was always a good option for a Carlisle Indian. Those minor-league and semipro teams were glad to have a Carlisle boy or two on their rosters. Everyone knew how talented our ballplayers were. They might turn out to be another Bender.

I guess most people these days don't know who Charlie Bender was, but he was sure famous back then. I first met him that spring of 1907. I was sitting at the training table when there was a commotion at the other end of the room.

"What's up?" I whispered to Ex, who was sitting across from me and had a better view of what was going on behind my back.

"Oh my stars," Ex said. "You are going to like this." Then he stood up and held out a hand toward the tall, tanned man who had just been brought over to our table by Coach Warner. "Look what the cat dragged in," Ex said.

"Hey," the man said, taking Ex's hand in that gentle way all Indians shake with each other. None of those white man, hand-crushing grabs to prove you're the stronger one. "Aren't they ever going to let you graduate from this place, Ex?"

Ex chuckled and turned toward me. "Ever hear of Charlie Bender, Jim?" he said. "Can you believe this string bean actually pitched in the World Series for the Athletics? Charlie, this Okie Indian boy is Jim Thorpe, who is going to make a name for himself."

Charlie Bender smiled. "I am sure he is," he said. He held out his hand to me and I stood up to take it. "Pleased to meet you, Jim," he said.

And I surely was pleased to meet *him*. Charlie Bender was a Chippewa Indian from Minnesota who had graduated from Carlisle in 1903. I don't mean he just left after putting in his eight years, like most Carlisle students did. He actually graduated. He was the best baseball player Carlisle ever had and he went on to play at Dickinson College, where he got a college degree. But that wasn't the end of it. The major leagues wanted him and he was hired by the Philadelphia Athletics, where he became their star pitcher. Not only did he win six World Series games, he was one of the most dependable pitchers in all of baseball for about fourteen years.

Charlie never forgot Carlisle, no matter how famous he became. He returned time after time to encourage our Indian ballplayers and share what he had learned with them. If there was ever an Indian athlete who was a real hero, Charlie Bender was that person.

Although Charlie stuck around for much of that week, helping instruct the baseball boys, I didn't see much of him. The one problem I had with track was that it took place at the same time of year as baseball. Pop Warner was the coach of both the baseball and the track teams, but he wouldn't let me try to play both of those sports at the same time. Pop made it clear to me on more than one occasion that he wanted me to concentrate on track as my only varsity sport at Carlisle. But playing baseball on campus during the summer was okay.

When July came around, we put together a pickup team and played ball off campus. I did some of the pitching and I wasn't bad at it, even though the best thing I did was run the bases. One fine summer day, we got invited to play a local team in nearby Hershey, Pennsylvania. That was a sweet day. After we won the game, they took us on a tour of the big candy factory there. They gave us bags of candy and let us fill our pockets, too. I made sure to bring home enough to be able to share it around the dormitory.

16

NOBODY TACKLES JIM

Before long, it was the middle of August. Much as I'd enjoyed the easy pace of the summer, I'd been waiting for it to end. I was just itching to try out for the football team. Everybody had been talking about what our football team was going to be like this year. It was going to be the best team ever. Not only was Pop Warner fielding his finest players who were already students at Carlisle, but he had also decided to use Ex, even though he'd already graduated. Strictly speaking, Ex was still a student and he was living on the Carlisle campus. The courses he was taking were special ones at Conway Hall, a local commercial college that was a prep school for Dickinson. Four other Carlisle football players, including our quarterback, Frank Mt. Pleasant, were doing the same thing, taking those advanced courses at Conway Hall.

Pop had also recruited the best Indian players from such schools as Haskell. Pete Hauser was one of them. Pete had been part of the Haskell team that was whipped by Carlisle by the score of 38–4 in a 1904 game that was the first and last time the two biggest Indian schools played each other. Pete was big and muscular. He had been the best runner and kicker on the Haskell squad. If it hadn't been for his kicking, the score would have been even higher in Carlisle's favor. His brother Emil, who played football at Carlisle under his Indian name of Wauseka, had also been on that Haskell squad. Wauseka was a lineman and he was even bigger than Pete. He just towered over everyone. The whole Hauser family was big and tough. Three of their sisters were also at Carlisle, and some said those Hauser girls were even tougher than their brothers.

What a lineup the fifty-four team members on our 1907 squad was! The center, Nikifer Shouchuk, was an Eskimo from up in Alaska. He was small for a center, short-legged and low to the ground. But he was just as ferocious as he was ugly. The joke was that he could knock people down just by looking at them. Nikifer's work assignment at school was in the kitchen and he had been the main cook through the summer. To be honest with you, we were glad to see him getting back into full-time football so we wouldn't have to suffer through his cooking anymore.

Little Boy, who had been kicked out of Haskell and banned from attending every reservation school in the west, was one of the guards. He was an example of how Pop Warner believed in giving a man another chance—especially if he could block and tackle. Afraid of Bear was the other starting guard. The tackles were Antonio Lobo—who was twenty-six years old and, like Ex, had played on Pop's first Carlisle team—and Wauseka. Ex got moved to end after learning how to run downfield and catch the passes that came spiralling off the hand of Frank Mt. Pleasant. Before Frank learned the right way to do it, a pass had been thrown like lobbing a big rock. But Frank used his fingertips to give the ball a spin, as all quarterbacks do today. William Gardner was the left end, who got almost as good at catching a pass as Ex.

Owl, Little Old Man, Cries for Ribs, Two Hearts ... just saying their names again gives me a chill. As Carlisle students in classes or in military formations, they had to use their English names. But when we stepped out onto the field, Pop Warner gave us the choice of using those older names that had such power. Part of it was that Pop was giving us respect by doing that. But I also know that another part of it was because he knew the effect those names had on the non-Indian teams we played. It reminded them who we were. Playing ball against a bunch of real, live Indians unnerved some of those white college boys. Pop Warner would do anything within the rules to give his teams an edge.

Some of the other teams we played that year complained that Pop Warner had ignored eligibility rules to build up our Indian powerhouse team. Pop countered by pointing out that fifty-two of our fifty-four team members were full-time students. That was at least as many as some of the teams we played. Only two of our members had played more than four years, which was the new limit in the east. And only one of our regular players was an employee. Back then, more than one college team used their coaching staff as players.

One other thing to remember is just how small Carlisle was compared to the colleges we played. Those schools had thousands of young men. Carlisle had about five hundred and only half of those at any given time were big and strong enough to even try out for football. It was really, like in that Bible story, David against Goliath.

Joining the football team wasn't just my idea. Plenty of other Carlisle students, in particular the other Okie Indians, had been urging me to take a shot. Mr. Newman, one of my favorite teachers and a great football fan, also strongly believed I should give varsity football a try.

"Jim," he said, "you are head and shoulders above the other boys on my intramural football team. I am certain you'll have success."

Now, in most cases you weren't even allowed to try out for the team without Pop Warner's permission. So Mr. Newman wrote a special note to the equipment manager, telling him that they should issue me a uniform so that I could try out.

That didn't sit well with Wallace Denny, the Oneida Indian boy who was the trainer for the football squad. He took one look at me and decided I was too skinny. He also knew I was one of the track boys and that seeing me on the field would not make Coach do cartwheels. So Wallace tried his best to discourage me. First he couldn't find any spare uniforms. Then, when I just kept patiently waiting, he fitted me out in an old jersey and pants that was three sizes too big for me. As I jogged out onto the practice field they flapped on me so much that I looked like a scarecrow in the wind.

I might have looked like a scarecrow, but Pop Warner didn't laugh. Instead, he looked like he was about to blow a gasket when he caught sight of me.

"What are you doing here?" he said, his round face getting red. Then he used a bit more colorful language. Pop had learned that we Indians didn't like swearing and so he tended to avoid those words as much as possible. But every now and then he just couldn't help it.

He took a deep breath. "I'm only going to tell you once, Jim. Go back to the locker room and take that uniform off. You're my most valuable track man and I don't want you to get hurt playing football."

But I didn't turn around. "Coach," I said, "I'm here to try to make the team."

Pop Warner had already learned how stubborn I was.

"All right," he said, "if that's the way you want it."

But from the little smile on his face I knew he had just come up with an idea that I probably wouldn't like. Sure enough, instead of anything that involved contact with the other players, he sent me off to the side of the field to practice kicking. Punts, field goals, dropkicks, kickoffs. That was all I was allowed to do for the next two weeks.

I was good at it, too. Before long, I was regularly hitting the ball through the goalposts from forty yards away and punting just about the whole length of the field. Kicking has always been a big part of football, and back then you could score four points for a field goal. You were also allowed to catch your own punt if you got downfield fast enough. I could have left it like that and made the team as a kicker. But that wasn't all I wanted to do. I wanted to run.

Jim, 1912

So I kept bothering Pop Warner about it. "Can I carry the ball now?" I'd ask, not just once, but again and again. I was like a mosquito that kept buzzing around his head.

Finally, Pop got so tired of being pestered that he decided to teach me a lesson. It happened when we'd finished our conditioning drills. Instead of going off to the side with the other kickers, I asked him that inevitable question again.

"Can I carry the ball now, Coach?"

He shook his head, picked up a football, walked over to the goal line, and beckoned for me to join him.

"Open field tackling practice," he yelled.

As soon as he did, the whole team ran out to take their places on the field. In those days, a football field really was a gridiron, with both horizontal and vertical lines that cut the field up into squares that were five yards on each side. Just like men on a checkerboard, every player took one of those squares. I knew this drill. My job as a running back was to run toward the goal at the other end. To get there, though, I had to run through more than forty tough football players spread out over the whole field.

Pop Warner slammed the ball into my stomach.

He didn't have to say anything. I took off like a jackrabbit. I sprinted past half of those football boys before they ever saw me coming and I ducked and dodged and just plain jumped over all the rest of them. Not one of them touched me. Then I trotted back and flipped the ball to Pop Warner. He was staring at me with his mouth open like he was trying to catch flies. I guess he didn't know if what I'd done was skill or just dumb luck. But he recovered his composure.

"Dang it," he said. "You were supposed to give them tackling practice." He looked down the field. "Don't take it easy on him, boys," he shouted. "You catch this rabbit!"

Then he looked over toward Ex, who was suited up like the others but had been on the sidelines. "You, too," he said.

Ex looked over at me, rolled his eyes up toward the sky, then ran out to take his place. I knew he sympathized with me, but I also knew he was going to try to hit me as hard as he could. And that was *hard*. Ex was known for knocking other players out of the game with good clean hits.

Pop Warner handed me the ball a second time. "Go again," he said, "and this time don't just run around everybody like a sissy."

That made me mad. I took off again toward the other goal line. And this time, although there were plenty of would-be tacklers who ended up grabbing nothing but air, I didn't dodge everybody. I lowered my shoulder, lifted up my knees, and either knocked tacklers aside or ran over them. When I turned to look back from the other goal line, the team was spread out on the ground like a forest of trees that had been knocked over by a tornado. Ex was among them, flat on his back, holding his empty hands up toward the sky and laughing to beat the band.

I trotted back to Coach Warner and handed him the football again. "Coach," I said, "nobody tackles Jim."

17

THE WORLD OF THE FOOTBALL BOYS

Being one of Pop Warner's athletes was a great thing at Carlisle, but being in the world of the football boys was even better. For one thing, as Ex put it, "Football boys eat high off the hog."

I suppose a lot of people these days in America just take it for granted that they'll have good food to eat. That was never the case for those of us who came up through the Indian boarding schools. Some of the poorer Indian schools had a hard time feeding their students even two good meals a day. Sometimes that was because the people running the school were stealing the money meant to buy provisions. The boys and girls at schools like that were fed stale bread and beans with only water to drink. Some of my friends told me how they used to sneak out to the stables at night to steal the corn that was for the horses, which were being fed better than the Indian children. When they finally got to Carlisle, even though the food was not great, it was like manna from heaven compared to what they'd had before.

For ordinary students at Carlisle, the meals might have been filling but they weren't much fun. Breakfast every day was coffee and oatmeal, with no milk or sugar. Once a week you got a meat pie, but the other six days the only thing to flavor your breakfast was gravy ladled from a bucket. Dinner was beans or hominy served with butterless bread and more of those buckets of gravy. Now and then you'd get a piece of ginger cake. If you wanted anything more to eat, you had to buy it off campus with whatever money you had saved up. One of the favorite stops for everybody was Frank Farabelli's fruit stand on North Hanover Street. No apple or pear ever tasted better than one you bought there after a week on Carlisle's tasteless rations.

You could say that compared to some I didn't have much to complain about as far as food went. I'd been lucky enough to always eat pretty well before coming to Carlisle. At Haskell the food had been simple, but there'd been plenty of it. At Garden Grove I'd had my meals made by my sisters and my stepma at home. During those years of being a low-paid laborer on my Outings, I'd also been fed good, even when I was eating in the kitchen. But when I became one of Pop's boys, my menu became almost as good as it had been back in those dear old days when I was at home and Ma was still alive.

And it also wasn't just the food that changed, but the setting we had it in. Pop Warner had been allowed to take over the old hospital building on campus to remodel it into the football boys' quarters. It wasn't done on the cheap, but at the cost of over thirteen thousand dollars! Pop had the money for it, though. The ticket revenue that was earned every season by the Carlisle football team was ten times that much. Sure, Pop had built himself a brand-new two-story house on campus for him and his family with some of the football money, but he also used those funds to make life better for us players in every way he could.

Which brings me back to those new football quarters that I moved into in 1907. Our rooms were bigger and more comfortable. There were pool tables for us to use, a music box, and even a reading room with comfortable chairs, stocked with all the regional newspapers that covered Carlisle football. We could go there and read about our games in the *Boston Herald* or the *Philadelphia North American* or half a dozen other papers.

Best of all we had our own cook and our own kitchen and a dining hall where we could relax and laugh and talk about whatever we wanted—which was, admittedly, mostly football. However, we sure spent just as much time eating as we did talking because that food was good! We had meat and milk and potatoes with every meal, and there was always butter for our bread.

The only time we got better food was on our long road trips. Once again, all paid for from the football fund. We were allowed to order whatever we wanted off the menus in the train dining cars and the hotel restaurants. Some of us even learned to like some pretty strange foods that we'd never seen before. Oysters, for example. When I first saw Ex slurp down one of those slimy things I just about gagged.

"You know who was the bravest man who ever lived?" Frank Mt. Pleasant cracked as Ex polished up the last of a dozen oysters on the half shell.

Ex smiled back at Frank. "First one who ever ate a raw oyster."

Since we football players weren't able to go on Outings to earn money, Pop made up for that. Ever since Superintendent Pratt, it had been the practice of the school to award every varsity athlete with not just that big Carlisle *C* but also a generous allowance. Every football boy was given from ten to fifteen dollars a month for expenses. You could also get what Pop called a "loan" if you needed it, although those loans were never expected to be repaid. It wasn't just the football players that got them. My friend Louis Tewanima, the long-distance runner, was always given loans whenever he traveled to take part in major invitational meets. In addition to our allowance, if we played especially well, we were also given direct cash bonuses.

That first summer of practice as a real football player is one I will never forget. Just as he'd done with track, Pop Warner assigned my friend Ex to teach me the finer points of blocking and tackling and all the rules that had to be obeyed.

Pop Warner kept close watch and more than that. In fact, sometimes if he saw someone doing things in a way that he thought was wrong, he would explode.

"What the blankety-blank-blank do you think

you're doing?" he would shout. "This is how you block a man!"

Even though he was thirty-seven years old, Pop was still as solid as a brick wall. When he demonstrated a block, you ended up on the ground feeling like that brick wall had just fallen on you!

Ex was also learning that August. He'd been moved from tackle to end and now had to be prepared to catch a football and run with it himself. We ran endless hours of drills, sprinting down the field to catch one of those passes that spiralled off Frank Mt. Pleasant's fingertips. Pop Warner was miles ahead of just about every other football coach in America that year. While most other quarterbacks were still lobbing the ball ten or fifteen yards, Pop had us training for fifty-yard pass plays. Every back was expected to learn how to throw a spiral and although, none of us got as good as our quarterback at it, we all soon became a double threat with a ball in our hands.

At first I had a little trouble holding on to the ball when I was tackled, and learning to catch a pass took some doing. Of course I got teased about that.

"Jim, you may run like a deer, but you catch like you got hooves!" Wauseka said as he grinned down at me after another of his bone-jarring tackles that knocked the pigskin out of my hands just as I was trying to gather in a pass.

"Don't worry," Ex said to him, pulling me up to

my feet. "I'm putting glue on my boy's hands for the next play."

The teasing, though, was good-natured and I knew I was a real part of the team. When the first game of the season came around, I was in the lineup as the second-string halfback behind Pete Hauser.

INDIAN FIELD

Indian Field. No other football field would ever mean as much to me. We never played our biggest games there, the ones that made our Carlisle Indians famous. Those games were played at places such as Harvard and Penn and Princeton, big schools with grandstands that could hold thousands of paying spectators.

But it was at Indian Field that every new season started, like that first season of mine in the fall of 1907. Indian Field was located between one of the school farms on one side, and the dormitories and the shops on the other, just a short trot away from our new athletic quarters. People came pouring in to take up every bit of open space close to the field. Although we might not have had the crowds at Indian Field we had at Ivy League schools like Harvard and Yale, we still had plenty of fans. In addition to the whole Carlisle student body, hundreds and hundreds of other people came. Above the main street in Carlisle, the game of the week would be billed on a big banner. And it wasn't just the local people. Pop always made sure that placards and bills for our home games were posted up all around the area, drawing in folks from Chambersburg, Harrisburg, Shippensburg, Steelton, York, and other smaller towns. Seats were set up on the hill east of the field, while some people watched from their cars in the free parking area farther up the hill.

Those first games were played against teams from the small Pennsylvania schools that were nearby. More often than not, those teams were more like sacrificial lambs than opponents. It was rare when one of them even scored. I remember one game I saw during my second year at Carlisle when I was still too undersized to even be noticed. Albright College from Reading was the victim. The game was called at halftime that Saturday after Carlisle was ahead 100 to 0. One hundred points scored in thirty minutes!

At one-sided games like that, the Carlisle band ended up getting as much attention as the football players. If I hadn't been able to play sports, I think I would have liked to have been in that band. They always looked sharp as a razor and they could play as good as any band in the land. It was really something to hear them do one of the popular songs of the day, like "Great Big Indian Chief Loved a Kickapoo Maiden." Using that to greet the arrival of a crowd of white spectators was like a private joke for us Indian students.

Sometimes the Pennsylvania teams that played us tried to make their own jokes about us being Indians, jokes we didn't find all that amusing. Like in 1905 when Carlisle played in Harrisburg at Dickinson College. Some of the Dickinson boys did a little skit before the game in which a student dressed as a cowboy pretended to scalp another Dickinson student wearing a headdress and a Carlisle *C* on his chest. The Dickinson fans thought that was pretty funny, but they didn't laugh so much when our side of the field brought out a dummy dressed in a Dickinson uniform. Every time we scored, an arrow was shot into the chest of that dummy. Six touchdowns and six field goals later, that dummy looked like a porcupine!

That first season of mine started against one of those local teams, Lebanon Valley. It wasn't the official season opener, but a warm-up game. So it was played not on Saturday, but mid-week. It was a gloomy day, cool and looking as if it would rain at any minute. Even so, we had a good big crowd rooting us on. The school band started playing and then the whole student body stood up.

> *Minnewa Ka*
> *Kah Wah We!*
> *Kah Wah We!*
> *Minnewa Ka*
> *Kah Wah We!*
> *Carlisle! Carlisle, Carlisle!*

That was the school cheer they used to greet us as we football boys came trotting onto Indian Field. Like a lot of our old traditional Indian songs, those words didn't have any literal meaning, but they sure captured the emotions we felt. If you have never heard eight hundred or more Indian boys and girls yelling that out, you just can't understand how thrilling and inspiring it was for all of us at the start of every game. It just made my heart leap. I felt as if no one could stop me that day.

And for the whole first half no one did. That was because no one had a chance. I rode the bench for thirty whole minutes. Albert Payne, who was a Klamath from Oregon, was the starting left halfback ahead of me, and Pop never took him out. By the end of the first half we were ahead 40 to 0 and it was raining hard.

When the second half began, Pop motioned me and the rest of the reserve backfield to go on in. I went in for Payne. Owl went in for Hauser at the other halfback and Bill Winnie went in for Hendricks at fullback. Louis Island, who was Oneida, went in for Mt. Pleasant. Poor Louis never managed to have any real success in football at Carlisle, and that first game was no exception. He had a hard time with the snap, and his ballhandling was sloppy. I only touched the ball a few times, and between the mud and the bad handoffs, didn't get all that far. I wasn't really knocked down by any of the Lebanon Valley boys. I either slid into them or was tripped up by my own players. After a few more minutes of that, Pop decided not to risk the chance of any of us getting hurt. The game was called.

I was a little disappointed, but I knew I could do

better. So I worked even harder when we was back practicing the next day for our real season opener. On Saturday, September 25, we'd play Villanova on Indian Field.

Villanova might have been used to going up against big teams like Yale and Penn and Harvard, but they were not ready for us Indians. Three thousand people watched the game that day as we took them apart with our running and our passing. Frank Mt. Pleasant not only played quarterback, he also received the kickoffs and he took that ball from one end of the field to the other like our opponents was standing still. Pete Hauser ran for one touchdown and caught another. Then he put a long field goal through the uprights.

Once again, when we were way ahead and it was late in the second half, Pop waved in the second team and I got to play. Frank Mt. Pleasant stayed in at quarterback. I didn't make any touchdowns, but I followed my blockers and gained yards whenever the ball was in my hands. And for the first time I heard something that I would always love.

"Thorpe! Thorpe! Thorpe!"

Led by all of my other Sac and Fox friends, my name was being chanted by the Carlisle fans.

19

FIRST TOUCHDOWN

Some folks have said, Pop Warner included, that our 1907 squad was the best football team Carlisle ever had. There's no doubt that we had speed and strength and skill, great balance at every position, and coaching like no other team. We beat the best teams that we played. At times we looked invincible, especially at home. It had been seven years since another team had scored a touchdown on Indian Field and we kept that streak going.

Good as our team was, though, that first year of football was far from my favorite. Despite the fact that I continued to do well in practices, my main role in far too many game days was to warm the bench with my backside. From my front-row seat by the sidelines I had a great view as our first-stringers beat up on those bigger players from Penn State. I cheered along with all the other bench riders when Ex gathered in the game-winning touchdown toss from Frank. But I never got a single second of playing time.

October 12 was the Syracuse game, played in Buffalo to take advantage of the bigger field. Having it there also meant that it was right between the Iroquois reservations in New York and Canada. Indians poured in over the bridge from Canada to see us play. It may be hard for people now to understand how important the success of our football team was to a lot of Indian people—people who knew nothing more about football than the fact that our all-Indian team was knocking the stuffing out of those white teams who thought they were the best. Indian people had lost so much by that time—their land, their ways of life, their languages, and even their children were being taken from them. Any kind of Indian victory was an inspiration for them, like a little glimmer from a distant campfire helping you find your way through a long, dark night. Crazy Horse was dead, Sitting Bull was dead, Geronimo was being held captive in Oklahoma. But on the Carlisle field, for an hour or two on cool fall afternoons, our little band of modern warriors was winning battles for the pride of every Indian.

There was even more Indians at that game because of Frank Mt. Pleasant being Iroquois and this being his people's homeland. Frank's Tuscarora Reservation was close by, not far from Niagara Falls. I think every Tuscarora that could walk made it to that game, and I expect that a third of them were Frank's relatives. I heard it estimated that twelve thousand fans saw that game. Because they were the ones who pressed closest to the field it seemed as if half of them were Indians. They were all around our bench and whenever a sub was sent onto the field he had to make his way through that crush of chanting, happy Indians. Sometimes all I could see from our bench was the tops of the helmets of our players—Ex's white helmet flying down the field like a bird, Pete Hauser's red helmet slamming its way through the line.

To help our quarterback keep track of his eligible receivers, our helmets had different colors on them. White was for ends. Red was for backs. That was another of Pop Warner's bright ideas—as were the pieces of leather that looked just like footballs sewn on the front of our jerseys. If you held your hands up to your chest as you ran, those leather shapes made it look at first glance as if you were carrying an actual football. That confused other teams so much as to who really had the ball that it was eventually made illegal. Of course, by then Pop had thought up new and different ways to keep opposing teams buffaloed.

It was one tough game. Syracuse tried everything they could to keep from getting beat, including slugging and tripping and piling on after the play was over. Frank was so elusive and quick that he was able to avoid getting hurt, and Pete Hauser was just too tough for them. Our other halfback, Albert Payne, though, wasn't as lucky. He took so much punishment that he had to be pulled out of the game. And guess who his replacement was!

"Thorpe," Pop Warner bellowed. "In for Payne!"

As I made my way through those shouting Iroquois, I got patted on the shoulder and thumped on the back so often that I felt like I'd already been getting tackled by the other side for a whole quarter by the time

I reached the huddle. And when I got there I realized that I couldn't remember a single play and I wasn't sure of the signals. I looked over at Ex and he understood.

"Just do what I say, Jim," he said.

And that was what I did. Before each play he'd tell me where to run, if I was going to take a pitchout, which blockers to follow, and so on. I managed to get through the rest of the game without making any big mistakes. I didn't fumble or get thrown for a loss. I ended up making a little yardage every time I got the ball, even if I never broke away or made a score. Pete Hauser was the hero of the game. He scored all the points for Carlisle, including the final score that put us ahead to stay at 14–6.

The week after that, against Bucknell on Indian Field, Albert still wasn't well enough to stay out on the gridiron. I was brought in in the first quarter. Pete Hauser took a break, too, and Theodore Owl filled in at the other halfback. Frank Mt. Pleasant also sat out the game. His quarterback slot was taken by Mike Balenti and Louis Island, who alternated plays.

Mike was tough-nosed and one of the smartest students at Carlisle. In fact, when the academic averages came out that fall, he was number two in the whole school. But he was miles away from being as good a quarterback as Frank. Louis managed to play better than he had before, but not all that good. Throughout the game, neither one of them did well in ballhandling. In situations where Frank would have passed us out of trouble, they resorted to dropkicks. In fact, Pop Warner was so unsure of his two second-string quarterbacks that he had limited them to only three running plays, which sent us backs either right, or left, or up the middle. So many of our first-stringers were bunged up that I did most of the ball carrying.

It turned out to be my most successful day yet. I broke away more than once for runs of twenty or thirty yards, even if the blocking of our patched-up line was weak and the pitchouts and handoffs were so bad that I got them on the bounce more than once.

My best play, though, was also my worst. Late in the second half, I took the kickoff, followed my blockers, and saw a clear lane. I cut around the end, slipped another tackle, crossed midfield. I was headed for the end zone and about to make my first touchdown. But at the ten-yard line a Bucknell player on my blind side made a desperate dive that caught me around my ankles. I fell flat on my face and the ball bounced out of my hands.

"Oh no!" I groaned just as I heard another voice yell, "I got it!"

It was Owl, who scooped that ball up and took it the remaining seven yards for a touchdown.

It ended up with us winning 15–0. The week after that, the article in our school newspaper about the game mentioned my performance on the football field for the first time.

Thorpe did most of the work carrying the ball and proved to be an excellent ground gainer.

That was what it said. It made me feel good, but not good enough to forget how bad it felt when I fumbled that ball. It was probably because of that fumble that I started off our next game, at Penn, on the bench again, even though Pete and Albert weren't yet at a hundred percent.

Penn was a Big game with a capital *B*. The University of Pennsylvania was an Ivy League school, and in those days the Ivys prided themselves on being the best of the best in everything, from academics to sports. Not only that, Penn was undefeated and some of the sportswriters were saying it was the best team in the country. There was no question in Pop Warner's mind that he had to have his best, most-tested players on the field.

Early on in the first period, though, Pete's leg hurt so much he had to limp off. Pop Warner looked over at the bench and shrugged.

"Thorpe!" he yelled.

I was so excited to be in another game that I forgot to follow my blockers the first time I took the pitch. I ran headfirst into a towering wall of Penn players. They came down on me like a ton of bricks and flattened me for a loss.

I learned my leason. The second time I got the ball, I hung back, watched the blocks, then went around the end. I was in the clear and this time nobody was going to catch Jim! Seventy-five yards later I was in the end zone, holding the ball over my head. I had scored my first touchdown!

Frank Mt. Pleasant was back at quarterback, and boy, was he back. Those poor Penn players hardly knew what hit them. Frank would drop into what they thought was a punting formation and then throw a fifty-yard pass. Penn lost by a score of 26–6, but that was only because we took it easy on them in the second half. We outgained them by 402 yards to 76 and had twenty-two first downs while they only managed three.

I had started keeping a scrapbook. I pasted into it a copy of the article that ran in the *Philadelphia Press* and mentioned my touchdown. One part of that article, though, shows how folks thought about Indians in those days. Even when we won, they didn't give us the same kind of credit they would give a white football team.

With racial savagery and ferocity, it read, *the Carlisle Indian eleven grabbed Pennsylvania's football scalp and dragged their victim up and down Franklin Field.*

Letdown. That is what happens sometimes to a team after winning a big game, especially as an underdog. To this day, I still have to shake my head in disgust when I remember the Princeton game. It should have been a great day for me, but it sure as heck was not.

Our game against the Princeton Tigers was played on the famous Polo Grounds in New York City. It was my first start at halfback and I couldn't wait. It was awe inspiring to be on the same field where the greatest baseball players in the world swung their bats. The crowd that came to see the game was so big and so eager to get close that it broke right through the wire fences. What finally held the fans back from the field of play was a circle of dozens of Pinkertons, hard-nosed men from the famous detective and security agency.

Folks had come there dressed as if it was a holiday. There were businessmen in suits and dudes in straw hats, society ladies in fine gowns and furs, pretty young belles bedecked in ribbons and feathers. Walter Camp, who chose which football players each year would have the coveted title All-American, was there. People were paying as much as seven dollars a seat, which was a huge price in those days. Everyone thought they were going to watch the new style of football that Carlisle played with long passes and thrilling runs.

New York City was a long way from Carlisle, too far for our fellow students to come to the game in great numbers. If any Carlisle students wanted to go anywhere off campus, even to a school sporting event, they had to pay their own way, and our students never had much spending money. But everybody at the school fully expected us to have another great victory, and they would be following our progress using a special telegraph link. Princeton had already lost some games that season and everyone in the whole country who followed football expected that our Indians would just run right over them.

What no one expected was the weather. It was awful. It started to rain even before the beginning of the game. As both teams took to the field, the Princeton boosters started up a cheer that could barely be heard because the rain was coming down so hard. But I made out enough of the cheer to know I didn't like it. Each verse ended with "Poor Mr. Indian."

Then it rained harder. It didn't just pour, it was like standing under a waterfall. Those fans in their fine suits and gowns soon looked like a flock of wet hens. After the first few plays, we looked even worse—coated with mud from head to toe. There was so much mud underfoot that I felt like I was running in a swamp. Passing was even harder because you couldn't even see the ball in the air. The *New York Times* got it right the next day when they reported that our team "played a headless game which failed to do justice to its real strength." The Tigers, who were bigger and heavier and not a team that relied on speed and long passes like we did, just plain ate us up. We lost 16–0.

Even so, Pop Warner was not completely disappointed. Our share of the game receipts was the most ever. When Walter Miller, the man Pop Warner had hired to be his financial clerk, reported the amount that was being deposited into the athletic fund, it made some of us gasp. It was a whopping $9,253, the equivalent of ten times that amount in today's money. Pop hated to lose, but that was some consolation to him. And he knew we'd be all the more anxious to prove ourselves the next weekend against Harvard.

That Harvard game was the very biggest game of the season for us. Harvard was *the* Ivy League school, the most famous and glamorous rival we had. It would be a real test of Pop Warner's system because every man on that Harvard squad outweighed us by a good twenty pounds. Not only that, Carlisle had never beaten Harvard before. In the ten previous tries, the Harvard Crimson had always come out on top.

By that weekend at Cambridge, our usual starting players were healthy. I found myself on the bench again along with Mike Balenti and Theodore Owl. I didn't like it much on the bench. But even if it looked like I wasn't going to get on the field, I wanted our boys to whip 'em in front of that crowd of thirty thousand screaming Harvard fans.

"Remember last Saturday," Frank Mt. Pleasant said to the line. And the way Frank played that day left no doubt that he hadn't forgotten our one defeat. Frank scored a touchdown on a seventy-five-yard kick return and then set up two more scores with long passes. Nobody seemed able to keep up with our ends, Ex and Bill Gardner, who just ran circles around those Ivy League boys. Our boys were so fired up that it seemed as if nothing could stop them.

"Speedy Indians Crush Harvard" was the headline in the *New York Times*.

That night, back at Carlisle, our students were allowed to hold a victory parade. The residents of the town cheered from their front porches as a long line of Carlisle students in their nightshirts marched through the town. They carried torches and a stretcher that held a crimson-sweatered dummy labeled as the "remains" of Harvard.

We had only two more games to go after that, both of them way out in the Midwest. We went by train and I guess that was the best part of the two weeks for me. I loved the dining car and the card games that we played as the miles whipped on past us. I'd been on trains before, but those had always been lonely journeys for me, usually taking me away from home. It was different with a bunch of buddies around, even if they did seem determined to play one joke after another on me and the other younger guys on the team. The first night I jumped into my berth I found out too late they had short-sheeted me, and the sound of me accidentally tearing my sheet in half was answered by a bunch of guffaws from the guys who did it. The next morning when I got up, all my clothes was missing from my Pullman berth. I had to go around the train in a blanket, retrieving a shirt here, a sock there.

It kept on when we got into our hotel rooms. By then I had learned to always check my bed before getting into it—the shaving cream under the covers had been worse than being short-sheeted. But when I went to pick up my shoes from the hall, where we'd been told to leave them to have them shined, I found that they were missing their laces. The next morning, the laces were in the shoes, but one shoe was a size 9 and the other was a 12. One night I was told to go downstairs to get a message from the lobby, which turned out to read, "Enjoy sleeping in the hall." Of course, when I went back upstairs I had been locked out of my room.

None of it was mean-spirited, though. It was just the kind of hijinks that everyone on a team has gone through. Nobody ever got hurt, and if anyone ever acted like they really were sad or feeling left out, the older guys was always quick to cheer them up.

Our first of the two Midwest games was against Minnesota. I got to start, and I didn't do too badly. But when it became clear it was going to be close, Pop pulled me out and put Payne back in. The final score was 12–10 in our favor. I had spent most of that game with my old friend, the bench. "You gave a good account of yourself, Jim," Ex said, but I felt like I hadn't even had a chance to get going.

The last game of the season was against the University of Chicago at Marshall Field. Once again, we had to go against an undefeated team, and Chicago was also the Big Ten champ. Frank Mt. Pleasant had suffered an injury to his passing hand that was worse than we'd feared. His thumb was broken. Mike Balenti had to start in his place. To make things even worse for us, Chicago's coach was Alonso Stagg, who was almost Coach Warner's match when it came to strategy. Coach Stagg had been studying our passing attack and came up with what he thought was a way to stop it. It was probably the first-ever pass defense.

From my front-row seat on the bench I watched Coach Stagg's strategy take effect. It was actually pretty simple. You can't catch a ball when you've been knocked down. Every time the University of Chicago players saw an eligible receiver, they flattened him. If he got up, they laid him out again. There were no rules then about waiting until the ball reached the receiver before you could hit him. Ex was bouncing up and down like a basketball from all the hits he took.

On the other hand, our boys shut down Chicago's biggest weapon—their kicking game. A field goal was worth four points and their star player, Wallie Steffen, usually made three or four a game. Whenever Steffen got the ball, Ex and Bill Gardner were right on top of him. He couldn't run or kick. He only managed one field goal in the whole game.

Two plays out of three, Pete Hauser carried the ball for us. He also kicked three field goals. We were ahead, but Chicago was far from beat. Then Ex came up with an idea. "Hold on to the ball as long as you can," he told Pete. "Then throw it toward the goal line."

As soon as the ball was snapped, Ex took off. Instead of running forward, he ran out of bounds, circling right behind the suprised Chicago bench before coming back in fair territory fifty yards downfield. Pete heaved his pass. Ex grabbed it and ran in for a touchdown.

Coach Warner was laughing his head off, but Coach Stagg just about blew a gasket.

"That receiver was ineligible," he yelled. The referees talked it over. There was no rule about running off the field during a play and coming back in again to catch a pass. The touchdown stood. The year after that, Coach Stagg pushed through the rule that going off the field and coming back on was illegal, but it was too late by then.

At one point in that game I thought I was going to get in. After a really hard hit, Bill Gardner started staggering around. It seemed like he didn't know where he was. I stood up to take his place, but Pop Warner waved me back and went to take a look at Bill.

"Can you play, son?" he said.

Bill couldn't say anything because his jaw was broken. But he nodded his head and stayed on the field. So the bench and I continued our old partnership as Carlisle went on to an 18–4 victory. Pop Warner said that Chicago game was one of the greatest victories he ever had. I was glad that we'd closed off the season in style, but I wished Bill could have stepped aside and given me the chance to get the ball one more time.

20
THE ASSOCIATION

Even though that season of '07 wasn't the best for me, it was great for our Carlisle Indians. We beat the best teams in America. My friend Ex made Walter Camp's All-American list. And we took in so much money in ticket sales. We'd made a bundle at Princeton, but that was nothing compared to the gate in Chicago. Pop's football fund got no less than seventeen thousand dollars from that last game alone. In all, our Carlisle Indian School Athletic Association had made fifty thousand dollars on those final four road games.

Since the association was chartered as a business, totally separate from the school, only the three-man executive committee—the superintendent, Pop Warner, and Mr. Miller (who was both Coach Warner's financial clerk and the treasurer)—could decide what to do with those funds. The Bureau of Indian Affairs had no say in the matter at all, and that was a good thing. I am sure there is no way the U.S. government would have agreed to the kind of spending that made the lives of the Indian students better and richer at Carlisle. Just like the money we were supposed to be paid for our allotments, they would have found some way to keep us from seeing a penny of it.

I knew that for a fact, having just spent a lot of time

and ink trying to get a little of the allotment money being held in trust for me. All I had asked for was fifty dollars to get a new suit, a hat, a watch, and some shoes. Considering the fact that my annuity and allotments brought in over five hundred dollars a year, I figured that wasn't much to ask for. Six months later I hadn't seen one penny or an accounting on the money being held in trust for me. They never even answered my letters. I guess they figured an ignorant Indian, even one going to school, couldn't be trusted with that much money. No matter that it was supposed to be his!

That wasn't just my experience. Every other Indian student at Carlisle who tried to find out about his or her trust money—or, heaven forbid, get their hands on a little of it—had the same thing happen to them. United States government–administered Indian money, it seemed, only belonged to the United States government.

The football fund at Carlisle was way different from that. It made us feel responsible and respected. All of us football players knew everything about the fund. Every student who earned a varsity C could come to the meetings and serve as an adviser. I've already told you about our new football dorm and the allowances and loans we all got from the fund. But that wasn't all that was done with the money. The lighting in the boys' and girls' quarters, a new hospital for the school, the school greenhouse, the printing offices, new staff cottages, and even the art studio were built with football funds.

Pop Warner was especially proud of that art building. The Leupp Art Studio was what it was called,
named after Francis E. Leupp, who was the new
national commissioner of Indian Affairs. Pop had
worked his own way through college by selling
watercolors he painted, so he loved the idea of training Indian boys and girls to do art. In the early days
of Carlisle, including when I first started there, the
only art Indians were encouraged to do was paintings
of trees and bowls of fruit. It was that way in all the
Indian schools, but Commissioner Leupp changed
things. Unlike the men before him, he thought that
some parts of our cultures were worth saving and
even promoting, especially art. He admired Indian
silverwork and other handicrafts. So in that new
art studio at Carlisle you could find Navajos making silver jewelry, Hopis weaving blankets, Lakotas
making lances, Chippewas beading moccasins, and
young people from all the tribes doing paintings of
things like buffalo hunting or traditional dancers in
full regalia.

I'd never seen so much Indian art in one place as
I saw whenever I walked through there. Before long,
though, you could find almost as much Indian art,
everything from paintings to moccasins, in Coach
Warner's home. Pop was a serious collector of Indian
art and one of the best customers of our student
artists.

He spent a lot of time in the studio, and not just
looking at things. He still did some painting himself

and he was always talking with the instructors, Angel de Cora and William Lone Star Dietz.

Miss de Cora was the leading American Indian artist in the whole country at that time and Pop had insisted that if football funds were going to be used to hire an art teacher they had to get the best. After football season was over, it wasn't at all unusual to find him in the studio talking with Miss de Cora about art.

Lone Star, who was half Lakota and half German, had been working his way through college out in Kansas by playing professional baseball and football when Pop hired him. Lone Star's father was an engineer and Lone Star was not only a talented illustrator but also a draftsman. Even better, he was one heck of a running back and smart as a whip when it came to football strategy. So Lone Star Dietz was an art instructor, a football player, and an assistant coach all rolled up into one.

It was all as good a deal for Lone Star as it was for Pop. In fact, it turned out to be an even better deal than anyone expected. Lone Star and Angel, who was young and unmarried and good-looking, worked so well together that, a few years later, they got married!

Football money went for other things, too. It paid the local ministers who came to run campus services every Sunday a weekly courtesy of five dollars. Whenever the local police caught a Carlisle student in town without a pass, it was the association that paid the police two dollars for bringing that boy or girl back to campus. We had so much money in the fund at the end of '07 that we decided to invest thirty thousand dollars in Northern Pacific and Reading Railroad bonds.

And, like I said earlier, because this success was owed to the blood and sweat of the athletes themselves, we not only helped decide what to do with the money, but we also got a share of the profits.

DOING WELL

One of the first things I did once I'd been given my share was get me that hat I had wanted. Mr. Mose Blumenthal, who was the local haberdasher, also fitted me for a new suit. He stepped back to admire his handiwork as I looked at myself in the mirror.

"In that suit you look like a real gentleman, Mr. Thorpe," he said.

"I sure hope so," I replied. Clothes make the man. That is what people said sometimes. Of course I knew no clothes would ever make me look like anything other than a mixed-blood Okie Indian. That was all right with me, just as long as that Oklahoma Indian looked like a man to be respected, somebody who was proud to be who he was.

I should mention that I didn't have to pay for that suit, which cost all of twenty-five dollars. It was a gift from Pop Warner, along with an equally expensive coat. Every single football player on the squad got the same, and our own charge accounts at Mr. Blumenthal's, too. I think we were his best customers.

We also attracted other business because all the local sports boosters would come into the haberdashery when we were there. That store really was our hangout downtown. Carlisle pennants hung from the walls along with pictures of Carlisle athletes. We were made to feel at home.

"Please," Mr. Blumenthal would say, "you just call me Mose, boys."

I tried to do that, but that old Oklahoma politeness kept getting in my way. Ma had always drilled it into me to show respect to my elders. So I still called him Mr. Blumenthal or "Sir" more often than not. Even though he shook his head when I did that, the little smile that came to his lips made me think he liked it.

The Chocolate Shop was another of the downtown places that was pure Carlisle sports. If you were a football boy, you could get a bite to eat there and put it on your tab. What made the place even more special was Mr. Arthur Miller, who worked for Pop as a public relations man. Colonel Miller, as everyone called him because of his service in the Spanish American War, had what he called his office there. It was a small booth with a single chair that just about held the colonel, who was not a small man. The table in front of him was always covered with press releases and photos that he sent out to the syndicate of more than 150 newspapers around the USA hungry for news of Carlisle's sports triumphs.

Pop Warner spent a good bit of time in the Chocolate Shop himself. I'd walk in and hear his voice call my name. "Jim, come on over here, pull up a chair." And there he'd be at the booth he liked to use. You could recognize it even when he wasn't there because whereas every other table had only one set of salt and pepper shakers, Pop's had at least a dozen. He'd use those salt and pepper shakers to work out plays. "It seems to me," he'd say, putting a salt shaker off to the end, "that if we move the left halfback over here . . ."

It was a great thing, being one of Pop's boys and part of the Carlisle system. To be honest, there were critics. The superintendent of Haskell publicly accused Carlisle of turning student athletes into professionals. And in November of 1907, Dr. Carlos Montezuma wrote an article that appeared in the *Chicago Tribune*. We all saw it, because it ran on the very same page as the coverage of the big Carlisle–University of Chicago game. I knew who Dr. Montezuma was, and not just because he was famous for his work on behalf of Indians' rights. I'd met him. Dr. Montezuma was an Indian himself and had been the school physician at Carlisle during Colonel Pratt's last years at our school. According to his article, which none of us agreed with, Pop Warner had led us all astray. I had liked Dr. Montezuma when he was our school doctor, but I sure didn't like what he said. He even had his facts wrong when he wrote that "on the 1907 team there were probably not more than one-third of the members who were in actual attendance at the school as students."

That was just plain untrue. The only one on our squad who wasn't in any classes at Carlisle was Ex, and he was taking college courses. You could be both an athlete and a top-notch student at Carlisle, like

Mike Balenti or Frank Mt. Pleasant. Not everybody on our team was as bright as those two, but to say we were just hired men was an insult to us.

Thinking of being a student, I was now enjoying all of my classes. Maybe it was because I was feeling better about myself, but they just didn't seem as hard as they used to. In literature, form and numbers, grammar, civics, and history my grades were all "Excellent," and I was doing just as good in my vocational work as a house and carriage painter. I was older than a good many of the other students in my classes and I found that they looked up to me. It was not just because I was an athletic boy, but also because I was serious about learning now. I would help out other students when they were having trouble in classes. My teachers took notice of that, especially Miss Wood, who was a freshman academic teacher. I did so well tutoring others in her history class that she did something extra special to reward my efforts.

"Mr. Thorpe," Miss Wood said one morning, "I am turning this class over to you for the day."

"Yes, ma'am," I said, without even blinking. I knew this lesson well. It was about the causes of the American Civil War and I'd first learned about it at Haskell. I picked up the book, went to the front of the room, and started teaching. The only hard point came when I looked out at the class partway through my lesson and noticed how attentively they were all listening to me. It made me think back to the way my brother Charlie had always looked when he was in school. His eyes had always been on the front of the room, his mouth open like he was hungry for every word our teacher said. Charlie's voice came back to me: "You can do it, Jim." I had to pause for just a second and wipe a tear from my eye. But I kept on with that lesson and did myself proud. Later on that day more than one of my classmates came up to tell me that I was a fine teacher and they wished I would take over our class more often.

What I was really looking forward to, though, was not teaching but the track season. Ex was in his last year of athletic eligibility that season, but he was also still spending just as much time as my coach. Under his guidance I learned even more about the running and jumping events I loved the best, especially the high jump and the hurdles. It took some doing, but I finally got the hang of flattening out my trailing leg and sailing over those hurdles one after another without touching a one. I felt like a deer gliding through the forest and leaping fallen trees without breaking stride.

My best event was the high jump. Coach Warner sent me to the Penn Relays in April and I won in the high jump with a leap of six feet, which was a height very few people could clear back then. When we went against Syracuse on May 14, 1908, Ex and I tied in the high jump, and I won both the 120 and the 220 hurdles. My best time that year for the 220 hurdles was twenty-six seconds, but I wasn't pushing myself.

That was the only criticism Ex ever had of me.

"You could break all the records if you pushed," Ex said.

But just winning was always enough for me. If I looked back over my shoulder when I was ahead and saw that the other boys were far behind I'd just take it easy over that last hurdle. Then I'd stroll over the finish line with a grin on my face. Racing the clock didn't mean much to me compared to racing other people.

Ex and I weren't the only successful people on that team of ours in 1908. Far from it. The person who usually won the broad jump was Frank Mt. Pleasant, who looked like he was a bird in flight when he took off. Walter Hunt was winning all the sprints. And little Louis Tewanima, who could never get a uniform small enough to fit his skinny body, was unbeatable in the long running events. With his shirt and his shorts flapping in the wind, he would leave the whole field behind whenever he ran the mile or the two mile.

May 30 was our last meet of the season. I competed in four events and I won the high jump and finished second in the low hurdles, the high hurdles, and the shot put. And now that track was over, I was free to follow another one of my loves—baseball. Carlisle played a twenty-seven-game schedule that year and they still had a few games to go. Now that the track season was over, Pop changed his tune about me not playing and he was glad to see me suit up for his baseball team. I was a right-handed pitcher. I tossed a shutout against Albright. And just as I used to do back in Oklahoma, I ran the bases faster and better than anyone else. I could squeeze a double or even a triple out of hits that would have gotten most hitters no farther than first base.

Baseball seemed to me like the sport that held out the most opportunity. There was no money in track or football, but a baseball player could earn a living at his sport. As I've mentioned before, the best Carlisle baseball players was always getting the chance to play in the summer leagues in between semesters. That spring Pop Warner gave everybody on the Carlisle baseball squad copies of a letter he had received from J. Frank Reidenour, the manager of the Hagerstown, Maryland, semipro team. It praised three of our Carlisle boys who had played for his team the previous summer.

"Never in the history of baseball in Hagerstown were three men connected with the team whose performance was so uniformly satisfactory as were these three boys—Balenti, Garlow, and Newashe—the past season."

Pop also had a letter like that from the Hershey semipro team. It was one of the options he hoped we'd consider for the summer. Although that year, being 1908, there was another kind of athletic contest that some of Carlisle's best would take part in. It was something called the Olympics, based on the ancient Greek games that took place about fifteen hundred years ago. The revival of the Olympic Games began in 1898 in Athens. Athletes from every part of the globe came to what was the world's biggest track meet.

"The best of the best will be there in Italy," Pop said to me. "You could be one of them, Jim."

I suppose I could have been. I also suppose I could have gone and played semipro baseball. To be honest, though, I wasn't much interested that year in either summer ball or the Olympics. That was not where I longed to be. I took part in the high jump in the 1908 Olympic trials, but I didn't do my best and wasn't chosen for the team. And that was fine by me. I knew where I wanted to go, and it sure wasn't overseas. I was ready to go home.

OKLAHOMA SUMMER

Oklahoma. That's a Choctaw word that means red earth. And, boy, was it great to see that red soil again when I stepped off the train in Oklahoma City. I'd been away for four whole years and I vowed to myself that I would never spend that much time away from my home territory again. Billy Newashe came with me, so it was two pairs of Sac and Fox eyes that were drinking in those wide plains, those small rolling hills. We stood there breathing in that summer wind that came whipping up across the land as if to greet us.

Neither Pop Warner nor the superintendent had been pleased to see us go. It wasn't unusual for a Carlisle student to head home for the summer and never be seen again in Pennsylvania. I guess every college student gets homesick, but when it comes to experiencing real homesickness—to the point where you like to die—us Indians take the cake. But Pop Warner agreed I should be granted home leave when I told him how concerned I was about my brothers and sisters, especially Mary, even though she was a grown woman. She'd had more problems than anyone deserved and I'll tell you more about them later.

"Also," I said, and this got a smile from Pop, "the fish in Oklahoma are missing me giving them their proper exercise."

Pop liked angling as much as I did and he didn't doubt I'd be catching my share of bass and catfish over the summer.

It had cost Bill and me $31.95 each for our rail fare, but we figured it was worth it to get back home. My older brother Frank was there waiting for us, just as he had promised in the letter I'd gotten back at Carlisle. I was surprised when I saw him, for he looked more like my father now than he had when we were young. It wasn't just in his face, but also in the way he carried himself. But he also looked tired and worn. The life of being an Indian farmer wasn't an easy one. Still, the smile that came over his face when he saw me took away some of that weight he seemed to be bearing.

"Little brother!" he yelled, grabbing me and just about breaking my ribs in a Thorpe-style bear hug.

Frank didn't have a wagon of his own, but he had managed to borrow one that he had hitched two horses to. They weren't a matched pair and only one of them, the black, was Frank's. I spent a little time getting to know them before we hopped on board. Like most Indian horses, they were ready to pull a wagon or a plow or carry a man on their backs. I planned to borrow that old horse from Frank whenever he would let me. I could hardly wait to get back into the saddle.

"So what's on your agenda?" I said to Bill as we left the station.

Bill leaned back and patted his stomach. "Breakfast, lunch, and dinner," he said. "I have been dying for my ma's home cooking."

I guess I ought to add that Bill Newashe wasn't kidding about that. I put on a little weight myself that summer, bulking up to 175 pounds. But when Billy met me at the rail station for our trip back to Pennsylvania, I hardly recognized him. His smiling, satisfied face looked like a balloon. He'd about doubled in size. I thought I was going to have to roll him onto the train. His sister Emma, who was at Carlisle with us, was so mortified when she saw him that she covered her face with her hands. To his credit, Bill lost most of that weight or turned it into muscle as one of our second-string linemen. By the time football season rolled around, he no longer looked like a Sac and Fox medicine ball.

I boarded with Frank and his Shawnee wife and their four children. Frank had a farm of thirty acres in Bellemont, which was to the west of our old homestead. It was close enough for me to ride over those hills on Frank's one old horse. Seeing those places where Charlie and I had spent so many happy hours made me want to laugh and cry at the same time.

"Wait up for me, my brother!" Did I hear that voice of Charlie's in the wind as I climbed down from the horse and looked across the prairie fields where we ran and played?

My little brother Eddie was more or less boarding with Frank and his family, too. Eddie was nine years old and attending the same Sac and Fox boarding school that I had gone to. He not only had that Thorpe look to him, he was in the habit of calling himself "Jim," not Ed. Somehow, I had become his hero. I didn't think I deserved it, but it made me feel proud having him want to take after me.

It turned out that he took after me more than I'd expected. Just like me, he was sent off to Haskell a few years later. And, just like me, he decided one day he'd had enough of it and ran all the way home from Kansas to Oklahoma!

My little sister Adaline was now thirteen. She was as bright as Charlie and just as pretty as Ma had been.

"They say I am extremely willful, Jim," she said to me after she had unwrapped her arms from around my neck.

"Well," I said, "are you?"

"I should hope so," she replied. That fall she was enrolled in Chilocco, which was another Indian boarding school up in the northern part of the state. Sure enough, she excelled in her classes, but when that rebellious Thorpe nature got the better of her, she just walked out one day and ran back to our Sac and Fox country.

According to Frank, our brother George was also working an allotment. He'd also married a Shawnee girl, but they were having some problems. We'd go over and pay him a visit later. And there were uncles and aunts and cousins who would be coming by or expecting me to call in. They had all been following my success in sports the past year and they were, as Frank put it, "as proud as Punch."

The one I most wanted to hear about was my sister Mary. Frank and all of us in the Thorpe clan were concerned about her.

"As usual," Frank said, "things are tough, but Mary is getting by."

When she was little, Mary had an accident. The result was that she wasn't hardly able to hear anything and her throat was so damaged that it was difficult for her to speak. She couldn't manage more than a harsh whisper. And when she did talk, it seemed like the only ones in the world who could fully understand what she was saying were me and Frank. I guess that is part of why she was so fond of us. In fact, when she saw me, she didn't just hug me, she picked me up off the ground and danced around with me.

"I'm glad to see you, too, sis," I said. "But could you leave me just one unbroken rib?"

Even though she was four years younger than me, Mary had already been married twice. Both of them was worthless men and neither of those marriages lasted more than a year.

"Isreal, duh ony goo tin I goh douda it," Mary whispered to me, as she patted the back of her son Isreal. I had to agree that he was one good thing Mary got out of her first disastrous marriage. His dad might have been a lazy drifter, but that little boy had his mama's strength and warmth. I knew that when I got the chance, after school was over and I'd found some way to make enough money, I wanted a family and lots of kids of my own.

I ended up spending as much time that summer with Mary and little Isreal as with all my other relatives combined. Despite the fact that she could hardly hear or speak and was unable to get much schooling, Mary was never made fun of by anyone. People respected and even feared her some.

We have this old game we play in Oklahoma that we call Indian football. Men and women play it together. The men can only kick the ball, but the women can pick it up and run with it. And there is plenty of blocking and tackling. Oh my!

Bill Newashe and I got into one of those games soon after we came back home. I took a look out over the field and noticed that my sister Mary had just arrived to take part in the game, too. That was obvious by the way some of the men who'd planned to play were suddenly remembering they had chores to do or places to go.

"Are you sure about this, Billy?" I said. "It's been a while since we've played. You know how rough our Sac and Fox girls can be."

"What are you talking about?" he said. "We're Carlisle football boys now!"

I just shrugged and didn't say anything else, not even when the ball got kicked over to Bill and he didn't see my Mary coming at him from his blind side. The sound of that collision just about loosened my molars. Bill was knocked flat and Mary was heading downfield with that ball in her arms to score a goal.

I went over to help Bill up.

"Jim," he said, "this Carlisle Indian is going to stick to college football from now on in."

It wasn't just Mary's physical strength that people respected. It was believed by most everyone that she knew how to use medicine. If someone tried to do her wrong, they'd find bad luck heading their way.

That was one of the best summers of my life. I spent time with my family, rode the hills on Frank's black, and did do a good bit of fishing as well. But that summer also got me to thinking. I saw how hard life was for every single member of my family. Oil was coming out of Indian ground now in Oklahoma, three million barrels alone from the Glenn Pool. But it seemed as if white men were getting all of the money and even the meager allotments for the use of our land weren't being paid to us. The city of Shawnee was growing in leaps and bounds from the oil money. But it had been made darn clear that half-breeds and Indians had to stick to their side of town, on the far end of East Main Street, if they didn't want to get beat by the police or jailed or worse.

That summer I took note of how Frank was working himself into exhaustion every day. He was growing cotton and corn on his thirty sandy acres, but he wasn't bringing in enough cash to save up anything. He didn't have a harrow or a cultivator or a wagon of his own. He needed a new plow and hoes and a full team of horses. I later wrote a letter to my guardian, asking for enough money to buy a wagon, which I planned to give to Frank. As usual, I got turned down flat.

When I went back to Carlisle that late summer of 1908, there was one thing I knew for dang sure. Pa had told me to show the world what an Indian could do. I was going to do that, and I was sure as shooting going to figure out some way to make enough money to help out my family.

WARM-UP GAMES

It was hard to go back to school after being home with my relatives, but I was looking forward to a football season where I'd be a starter. What I wasn't looking forward to, though, were the rules I had to put up with at Carlisle. It turned out that they were even worse than they had been before. Our new superintendent, Mr. Friedman, had made some changes, and I didn't much like them. No one did.

During his first year in charge, Superintendent Friedman had noticed how us Indian students sometimes missed classes or engaged in what he called "dawdling about" on campus. He figured he would put an end to that. Every student was given what he called a calendar card. Those cards listed what classes you were in and where you were supposed to be. Every student had to have those cards on them all the time and be ready to show them to any teacher or school employee.

Another unpopular move of Superintendent Friedman's was to cancel all our social receptions. All the students had enjoyed those get-togethers, where boys and girls could talk to one another, where there was music and we could even dance together.

As a football boy, I wasn't as affected by the new

rules as some were. When it came to what happened to his players, Pop Warner had the last word, even more so than the superintendent. If any football player ended up in the guardhouse, Pop would just send his secretary down with a note authorizing his release before the game.

I could hardly wait until our season opener on September 19. Conway Hall, the prep school for Dickinson College, came to Indian Field to play us. Our band was already on the field, their red and gold uniforms shining in the autumn sun as they marched. I could hear the sound of their drums and horns as I suited up. I thought about what I wanted to do that day as I flipped my hip pads back and forth a few times in my hands before sticking them into place.

Those "hair pads," as they called them then, were the lightweight ones that Pop Warner himself had designed. They said "Spalding" on them because Pop had sold the design to A. G. Spalding and Bros. back in 1903. It was the same with my knee pads and ankle braces. Pop designed them, Spalding produced them, and both sides made money on the deal. The Spalding Company was a great friend of Pop Warner and Carlisle, taking out ads in our school publications and running pictures of our football teams in their annual *Intercollegiate Football Guide*.

Some of the other boys were limbering up, banging their shoulders against each other, jogging back and forth. I'd do some of that on the field, but mostly I was just relaxing my body, getting ready to do what I saw myself doing in my mind.

Instead of me, though, Pop started Al Payne at halfback. I'd been doing a lot better than Al in practices, but Pop was rewarding Al, since he was a returning senior who'd held that slot last season. And, after all, this game was one of the three warm-ups before our schedule really got rough.

A few plays into the game, though, Al took a knee to his stomach and got the wind knocked out of him. Pop gave me the nod.

"In for Payne."

I went in for pain, all right, but the pain wasn't mine. The first time I got my hands on the ball, I went through the Conway Hall line like it was made of tissue paper. I didn't stop until I was in the end zone. After I scored four more touchdowns running and threw a touchdown pass to Pete Hauser, Pop pulled me out of the game. It was still only the first half and he wanted to make sure his new star halfback wouldn't get hurt.

The next game at Indian Field was Lebanon Valley College. Our boys and girls were all gussied up in their finest, as they always were for our home games. The boys had on suits and the girls wore their best dresses. Big hats were all the fashion for women in those days and some of the ones worn by our Carlisle girls were about as big as a boat with feathers and decorations on them. Well dressed as they were, it didn't stop them from yelling out our school cheer so loud it just about deafened the Lebanon Valley team as they approached the gridiron.

Pop's publicity machine had been working overtime, so Lebanon Valley had heard plenty about what happened to poor Conway Hall. I imagine it must have been pretty scary for them as they made their way onto a field surrounded by our enthusiastic student supporters screaming "Minnewa, Minnewa, Minnewa Ka, Carlisle, Carlisle, Carlisle!" Those players from Lebanon Valley stepped onto the field like lambs going to the slaughter. Once again, I was able to run pretty much as I liked and on my kickoffs I sailed the ball right through their end zone. Just like the game before, our second-stringers got to play as much as our starters.

The Villanova game, though, started off a lot tougher. Pop held me out of the game.

That didn't sit well with our fans. "Thorpe!" they yelled. "We want Jim!"

Pop ignored them. Figuring not to use me much until we started the hard part of our schedule on October 3 against the Nittany Lions of Penn State, Pop wanted to see what the rest of our team was capable of. Well, what he saw was not that good. Frank Mt. Pleasant had graduated and Mike Balenti was now the starting quarterback. Mike did a fair job of handling the ball, but didn't have Frank's speed. Nor could he make decisions like Frank, who always seemed to know when to hand the ball off or run or pass. Back then, coaches were not allowed to direct their team from the sidelines, so a quarterback had to think fast and keep a level head from one play to the next.

I guess I should add that being told he wasn't allowed to do something didn't necessarily keep Coach Warner from doing it anyhow. Pop was striding back and forth on the sidelines, waving his arms, slapping his legs, scratching his nose, and wiping his brow. It wasn't that he was nervous. What he was doing was secretly signaling in the plays with a private code that only our team knew. I believe he was the first coach to ever do that. Though he wasn't yelling instructions, Pop was still in charge of what was going on.

But even with Pop's signals, Mike was having a hard time. It wasn't just his fault. Our blocking was weak and our players kept fumbling. Villanova could not get past the middle of the field, but neither could we. It was late in the last quarter and still 0 to 0.

"We want Jim. We want Jim."

That chant from the Carlisle fans had been going on for most of the second half, but it was getting even louder now. Finally Pop sighed, walked over, and tapped me on the shoulder. I was off that bench like a shot. I don't think my feet even touched the field before I reached the huddle. We were on our own thirty-yard line.

"I get the ball," I said to Mike Balenti.

"You bet," he answered.

We lined up and I got the handoff. Instead of going

around the outside, though, I took another route. I'd already picked out the Villanova lineman who looked the strongest. I lowered my head and ran into him. *BAM!* And right over him.

"Out of my way!" I yelled, lowering my shoulder as I slammed the next would-be tackler aside.

After that, some of those Villanova players did get out of my way. Not that it mattered. I knew where I was going and nothing was going to stop me from getting there. I was running so fast that none of my blockers could get ahead of me as I went the whole seventy yards for the touchdown. Just like that, the score went to 5–0 and the game was ours.

Pop pulled me out. I'd broken the spirit of Villanova and he wanted me healthy for the games to come.

24

THE TOUGHEST SEASON

Thinking back on it, that year of 1908 was the toughest season of football I ever had, even though it had started off so well for me. October 3 was Penn State. That was our first away game, played in Wilkes-Barre. They managed to get a touchdown on us, when they blocked a punt and then ran the ball in. But we controlled the rest of the game and I did all the scoring, kicking three field goals to make the final 12–5.

Syracuse was on October 10, another game on the opponent's home field. The papers were full of the news that the Orangemen had whipped Yale. Carlisle's Indians were about to get massacred. Pop countered with his own publicity campaign. Instead of telling the reporters how good we were, he went the opposite way.

"Carlisle is a beat-up team," he said, shaking his head sadly. "My boys just don't have what it takes to beat a power like Syracuse. They are demoralized and out of shape."

When we took the field at Syracuse, we looked as bad as Pop had described. You'd think we'd all been in a train wreck. We limped out with our heads bandaged and our fingers wrapped with so much tape it looked like we were wearing white mittens.

We grunted and groaned and staggered through our warm-ups like a squad of seventy-year-olds. But when it came time to really start the game we pulled off all those fake bandages and showed those surprised boys from Syracuse what we really had. We shut them out, 12–0.

We didn't know it then, but we'd just about reached the high point of our season. The Susquehanna game on October 17 got canceled. The hardest part of our schedule—all road games—started on October 24 when we went to Philadelphia to play the University of Pennsylvania. Unbeaten, they were regarded as the best team in the country and deserved every word of praise they got. They had three times as many players as we did with talent at every position, including two All-Americans. The best of them was Bill Hollenback, their quarterback, who was also the fiercest tackler I ever ran into in my life. No matter what play Pop called, those Penn players knifed right through our line and got to the ball almost before we did. They scored on their first possession and then stopped us cold when it was our turn. Boy, did we get stopped cold!

I'd always been able to sidestep most players or fake them into making foolish dives, but not Bill. When he came at me, it was just a question of how hard he'd tackle me. When he did hit me, it was like being struck by a battering ram. I quickly learned that if Bill Hollenback didn't pulverize or half paralyze you with a head-on hit, you still played with a shaky feeling for the rest of the game.

What saved us in that game was that for once we held on to the ball. Penn was the team that fumbled. They lost the pigskin eight times and it kept us in the game, even though we trailed 6–0. Finally, in the second half we were on the Penn forty. I was tossed the ball. I saw an opening, sliced through, somehow got past Bill Hollenback, and scored. Mine was the only touchdown scored against Penn that whole season. I kicked the extra point and we were tied 6–6. That was how the game ended.

That was, without a doubt, the toughest game in all my years of football. I'd gotten not only a touchdown, but also a badly sprained ankle out of it. As a result, when we went to Annapolis to play Navy on October 31, I really *was* limping like an old man. I couldn't even kick the ball and didn't get to play at all. But we still won 16–6. Mike Balenti kicked four field goals. That surprised the heck out of Pop. Mike had never kicked before and two of those field goals were for more than forty-five yards!

"Where did you learn how to make those kicks?" Pop asked him.

"I just watched how Jim does it," Mike said.

Our next game was at Harvard. It was a bad one for us and this time kicking was what lost it. Back then, if a team punted the ball and their side got to it first, that ball was theirs. That was what happened to us on Harvard's first kick. They recovered it and ran it in for their first touchdown. Whenever we had the ball we did fine on end runs and line smashes and long passes, moving down the field every time. I had one fifty-five-yard pass play and a sixty-yard run. It even said in the papers after the game that "Carlisle played some rattling good football." However, we couldn't seem to get a score, even from the two-yard line. My sprained ankle still wasn't quite right, but Pop had me try eight field goals. Every one of them either missed or was blocked by the Harvard players. That made me feel lower than a snake's belly. Maybe it would have been better if Mike had still been kicking. We lost 17–0.

November 4 was Western Pennsylvania University in Pittsburgh—another hard contest. The weather was as tough on us as the other team. It rained like Noah's flood and the field was a mud pit. Kicking was impossible. But at least I was able to do something for the team this time. The only score in the game came when I ran off right tackle and took it into the end zone, winning the game for Carlisle.

Back then, we didn't have a set schedule far ahead of time for every week of the football season. We picked up games wherever we could and sometimes that was only a few days before we played them. A lot of teams still didn't want to go up against Carlisle, knowing that our Indians were such a rugged bunch. As the end of the season approached, Pop began trying his darnedest to get some more games. Our revenues from ticket sales were way down from the previous year. We'd made fifty thousand dollars in '07, but we'd be lucky to take in half of that in '08.

What Pop came up with was a western swing that

would take us to play in four different states in just fifteen days. Our grueling season thus far had left us feeling tired and beat up, but we still trudged onto the train that would take us first to Minneapolis—our second loss of the season, this time to the University of Minnesota. We just didn't play well and they beat us 11–6. St. Louis was next. We'd recovered some by then. I did most of the damage in the scoring and that ended as a 17–0 victory for Carlisle.

Not everything about that trip was a hardship. Life on the train was good. The food was terrific and we enjoyed ourselves playing cards and horsing around. As a star second-year player, I was no longer the butt of the practical jokes and got to play some of my own on the younger boys. By December 2 we were in Nebraska and feeling like our old selves again. I'm not sure how many yards I racked up, but I went through those Corn Huskers like they were corn stalks. Final tally: Carlisle 37, Nebraska 5.

Our final game, the thirteenth of that long, long season, was against Denver, the champions of the Rocky Mountain League. I had never seen anything before like those Rocky Mountains that just kept rising up along the railroad tracks until they blocked out the cold December sky. We'd been rising up, too. Denver was the Mile High City. By the time our Union Pacific train pulled into Denver, many of us had headaches from the altitude.

To top it all off, it was cold and snowing in the city. And it was worse on the field. The sod was frozen as hard as stone and the wind and snow was whistling around us. If they had told me it was Alaska, I would have believed them. I fumbled the ball and then got shaken up so bad when I hit the ground and the whole Denver team piled on top of me that we had to call a time-out for me to leave the game. Pete Hauser ended up doing the kicking. His two field goals made it possible for us to end that tough season on a winning note by the score of 8–4.

Much as I love football, I breathed a sigh of relief when that season was finally over. I was set to leave Carlisle for good and it wasn't just because of all the aches and pains I was feeling. The payments and loans that Pop ended up making to us players were pretty small, only about twelve hundred dollars total to be divided between us. Just as Pop feared, we'd ended up short on ticket sales that season. Then, shortly after New Year's, Pop called the team together to make an announcement. The entire policy of giving loans and cash gifts to Carlisle athletes was over and done. There had been too many complaints about it from other teams. Pop wanted to put an end to the bad publicity.

Considering all the hard work and pain and sacrifice it took to be a Carlisle Indian, that didn't sit well with me at all. I still had plenty of school spirit and I was proud of what I'd accomplished. But enough is enough. I wasn't one of those rich boys from *Hahvahd* or Yale who didn't have to sweat to make ends meet. By May I'd have done my five years at Carlisle. I needed to think about making a living, earning money so I could help out my relatives back in Oklahoma. And I had me a plan.

From here on in, I thought, it's baseball for me.

25

THE RELUCTANT TRACK STAR

Carlisle had hired a new baseball coach for the 1909 season. There was a schedule of thirty games. I planned to be playing in all of them. If I had as good a season in baseball as I'd had in football, I'd attract the notice of the major-league scouts. Joe Libby, who was also a footballer, was excited about our prospects.

"It's going to be a great squad," he said. "Mike Balenti's playing and Billy Newashe and Jesse Youngdeer. With your pitching and baserunning, nobody should beat us. Then when summer rolls around we'll get some great offers, for sure."

That sounded good to me.

However, as usual, Pop Warner had other plans. Now that he no longer had to coach baseball, he was figuring on making our track team a real national powerhouse. He called me to his office for a heart-to-heart talk.

"Jim," he said, "you know we need you on the track team. After all, that's where you got your start here. Plus you'll be captain of the team. You can wait until the end of the track season and still play the last few games with the Carlisle nine like you did last year. You'll have the whole summer ahead of you for minor-league baseball after that."

It was never easy to say no to Pop. He was as much a force of nature as he was a coach. Being stubborn myself, I understood Pop. Add into that the fact that I truly liked him and hated to disappoint a friend, and you know what my reluctant decision had to be. But it still affected the way I felt about school.

To tell the truth, since the turn of the year I'd been finding life at Carlisle a whole lot less fun. The superintendent's new system of making us carry schedule cards galled me so much that I started skipping classes out of rebellion. Sampson Burd, who was a Blackfeet from Montana, felt pretty much the way I did. He was an athlete like me, about the same size and weight. Also like me, Sampson's ancestry was a mixture of white and Indian blood. Folks kidded us about being twins, and we sure were that in terms of how we responded to those new attendance rules.

"Feel like a little vacation, Jim?" Sampson would say.

You know what my answer was. Away we would go on a little unauthorized jaunt off campus. If you were gone from the Carlisle grounds for more than a night or two, they would mark it down in your permanent record as "Ran." Our first run was in February, though we came back after three days. We did it again in March for four days, earning another "ran" in our reports.

Despite that, my final marks that year in deportment, dormitory, and industrial training were all "Good," while Sampson was "Fair" and "Poor." Being a star football player paid off for me, I suppose. Plus, even though I was bored with schooling, I was never rude to anyone, treated all my teachers with respect, and did pretty well whenever I did go to classes.

Track was better than being bored, and once the season came, I threw myself into it. At the Georgetown University meet, I won gold in the fifty-yard dash, the hundred, both hurdle events, the shot put, and the high jump. At the Carlisle-Syracuse dual meet in May, I took four golds, one silver, and two bronzes. Pop had developed a strategy on how to use me by then. He would have me do my running and jumping events first. Then, depending on how our other boys

Jim, left, racing in the 120 High Hurdles, 1909

were doing, he would send me over to the weights, where I could be counted on to win or place in shot and the hammer.

I wasn't the only one picking up fistfuls of medals that spring. My little Hopi buddy Louis Tewanima really came into his own. There was no finer distance runner in the country. Starting off in January of 1909 in New York at Madison Square Garden, in what was billed as "the biggest ten-mile race indoors ever," Louis outdistanced everyone. The only ones close to him at the end of a race were the two other Hopis on our team. He wasn't just winning in the five mile, the ten mile, the fifteen, and the twenty, he was setting world records. Running was Louis's life at Carlisle. Even though he was technically a prisoner of war, he had plenty of pride. He wasn't about to let anyone beat him. He was always training and trying to get better. Pop described him as the hardest-working athlete he'd every coached.

Louis did have a narrow escape in New York, though. Pop put Louis and the two other Hopis together in the same hotel room for the night after the race. They'd never been in a hotel before or seen a gas-powered light. When they were ready for bed, they blew out the light, just like they would do with their candles or kerosene lanterns back home. Pop hadn't thought to explain to them that the light in that hotel room was to be turned off with a switch. Even though the flame was blown out, the gas kept coming and filled up the room.

When Pop walked by their room the next morning, he smelled the gas and busted in the door. All three of them looked like they were dead and they surely would have been if they hadn't left the window partly open. As it was, it took Pop and the hotel doctor a long, scary time to bring them around. From then on, whenever Louis stayed in a hotel, even in the middle of winter, he always slept with all the lights on and the window open!

As good as I was doing, halfway through the track season my mind turned to baseball again. Just as Joe had said, our Carlisle nine was having a great season with our new coach. Pro scouts were looking at our best players. I wanted to be part of it. We were on a train coming back from a meet when I decided I'd had enough. I walked over to where Pop was sitting and writing something on a pad—probably a new play for next year's football season. He looked up at me standing there in the aisle and put down his pencil.

"What it is, Jim? " he said.

"Shucks, Pop," I said, "I'm through with track. It's baseball for me."

Pop reached up and took me firmly by the arm. He drew me down into the seat across from him. "Jim," he said, "you're not just doing track for yourself. Think of the duty you owe to your school and to your people. You are showing the world what an Indian can do."

Those were my pa's exact words and I didn't know how I could answer them. I heaved a deep sigh. "Oh, all right then," I said, "but I'd rather play baseball."

So I finished off the season, winning more golds and bringing that much more fame to Pop and the Carlisle sports program. Near the end of the track season, I joined my buddies Joe and Mike and Billy to play some games on the baseball team just like

Pop said I could. I didn't get seen by any scouts, but I did just fine, including a 1–0 shutout that I pitched against Millersville State.

Then it was the end of the semester. My five years was done and I was ready to move on. Of course, Pop Warner was planning on having me come back in the fall.

"Jim," he said, "you still have two more years of eligibility for football. These could be your greatest years."

But, like I said, I was tired of school. And now there was another thing. Carlisle was going to drop baseball entirely. Too many Carlisle boys were being distracted by its promise of summer jobs and the hope of becoming a star like Charlie Bender. The charges of professionalism were bothering Superintendent Friedman. With no baseball squad, there'd be fewer scouts trying to lure Carlisle boys into minor-league ball each year.

Having no more baseball at Carlisle would be fine as far as Pop Warner was concerned. Pop did love baseball and had once dreamed of playing in the majors himself before he threw his arm out in college. Pop was the one that baseball scouts talked to first when they were interested in Carlisle athletes for their summer leagues. But baseball at Carlisle led his Indian boys to dream about being professional players and that had become a nuisance to Pop Warner. Not only did it take their minds off of running track for him, there was the danger they might leave Carlisle entirely and not come back. I guess I became the prime example of that.

Mike Balenti was heading out to Minnesota to play for the St. Paul Apostles. Billy Newashe was going to Atlantic City, where he would play for a hotel team in exchange for room and board and tips. I might have joined them, but then Joe Libby and Jesse Youngdeer got what I thought was a better offer. A new team called the Rocky Mount Railroaders had been formed in the Eastern Carolina League. Pop Warner was actually the one who told Joe about it. That league needed some star players to build attendance. Joe and Jesse both signed to play. Fifteen dollars a week. "Come on with us, Jim," they said. "Possum is going, too. Once they see what you've got, they'll give you a contract on the spot."

"Sounds good to me," I said. "I guess I'll tag along."

First, though, I went to see Superintendent Friedman. "Sir," I said, "I wish to request a leave to play summer ball."

That didn't please him. It was just three days after the big Middle Atlantic Track Meet in Philadelphia. He had taken note of the fact that I'd scored twenty-five points for Carlisle there. That was more than any other athlete on any of the competing teams. The superintendent was a real track fan, even more than football. The thought of Carlisle's star track man running off to play baseball worried him as much as it did Pop Warner.

"Mr. Thorpe," he said, "you already took a summer leave last year. The understanding was that you would return and complete your studies. You have not done so. You have only completed your sophomore year."

"Sir," I said again, "I plan to play summer ball this year and I wish to request a leave."

Superintendent Friedman looked down his nose over his glasses at me. He could see I had my mind made up. He knew how determined I was. No matter what he said, my reply was going to be the same.

He sighed. "All right. You will be granted a summer leave to play baseball in the South." And that was what they wrote in my permanent record.

SUMMER BALL

Summer ball was what we called it. Back in 1909, there was a lot of it. There were no less than thirty-five different minor leagues to choose from. It was fun, but it wasn't exactly profitable. The fifteen dollars a week we earned was just enough to cover room and board and leave a little spending money. Two dollars a day. Shucks, Pop Warner gave us more than that when we were student athletes at Carlisle.

And if you'd seen Rocky Mount, North Carolina, you sure as shooting would not have called it the big time. The Rocky Mount Railroaders were based out of a tobacco town—the tracks of our Atlantic Coast Line train had passed through big fields of broad leaf on the way. The New Cambridge Hotel, where most of the baseball players stayed, was within sight of the little wooden station. Five short small-town blocks away was the stadium—if you could call it that. Most of the college baseball stadiums were bigger and a lot better kept than the one at Rocky Mount. All that the Railroaders had was a little covered stand behind home plate and a set of open plank bleachers down the left field line. The games they played were against squads from the other little towns along the rail line. The Fayetteville Highlanders, the Raleigh Red Birds, and the other teams from Goldsboro and Wilmington and Wilson were a far cry from the Yankees or the Red Sox. Rocky Mount was Class D ball.

"Welcome to the big leagues," Joe said as we stepped off the train. We all got a chuckle out of that.

I soon joined Joe and Jesse on the Rocky Mount team. The team manager knew who I was, not just from what Joe and Jesse told him, but from Pop Warner, too. He offered me a contract of my own, at that same fifteen dollars a week, to play third base. I took it.

My first game was June 15, 1909, against the Raleigh Red Birds. I was brought in at the start of the sixth inning. I had two at bats and struck out both times. We lost 5–1.

"I heard you can pitch," the manager said to me after the game.

"I guess you heard right," I replied.

Next day, against Raleigh again, I was the pitcher. I only allowed five hits and one run. I also got two hits of my own, one of which was a bunt down the third-base line. We won 4–1 and my name got into the *Raleigh News and Observer* for what would be the first of many times.

Thorpe, the Carlisle Indian and All-American halfback, proved to be very effective in the box.

Maybe we weren't getting paid much and it was hard to take those games seriously, but it was great to see your name in the news when you won. And we were real heroes to a good many in that little town. Each day before we played, kids would gather in the street outside the New Cambridge Hotel, waiting for us ballplayers to come out in our uniforms to walk to the park. Each boy sought the privilege of carrying the shoes or the bat or the glove of one of us ballplayers. I always made it a point to talk to those boys.

"How are you doing, sonny?" I'd say.

Then I'd ask them if they wanted to play ball some-day themselves. It took me back to the time when I was a little boy at Carlisle looking up to Chauncy Archiquette. He had looked ten foot tall to me back then. I guess we must have seemed that way in the eyes of those little kids. When we reached the park and they would hand me my bat and my glove, I'd always thank them and pat them on the back. You should have seen how their eyes glowed! I'll tell you this, a man who doesn't have the time to say a kind word to a boy is not worth a lick.

Fifteen dollars a day was enough for me to get by that summer, but I was not living high on the hog. I wrote to my Indian agent at the Sac and Fox Agency, Mr. W. C. Kohlenberg:

Will you please send my annuity and lease money here at Rocky Mount where I am stay-ing for the summer? If you have sent money to Carlisle, please recall it for I am not at school anymore.

Resp, James Thorpe

As usual, it was like whistling against the wind. My annuity and lease money got sent to Carlisle. Meanwhile, players came and went on the Rocky Mount team like it was a revolving door. I kept on pitching and running the bases better than any other player. They were calling me the "iron man of the league." Maybe that was because I tried harder than a lot of others did. Sadly, some of our other players even seemed at times as if they were deliberately trying to lose. The rumor was that it was because they'd been paid off or were betting money on the other team. There was some underhanded dealings, for sure, in the Carolina league. At some of our away games the balls that got thrown to us had been doctored and the umpires made bad calls in the other team's favor.

I never bet money on another team and I never took a bribe. A ballplayer who does something like that is as low as a snake. But, considering the kind of ball we were playing, I did sometimes just lay back and goof off a little now and then. I'd grin at the fans and crack jokes that would get everybody in the stands to laughing.

One game, when I was on the mound, my catcher called a time-out and came walking out to me. I'd been doing okay, but he thought I could do better.

"Thorpe," he said, "that pitching of yours is just slack! You have got to throw harder!"

"Are you sure of that?" I asked.

"Throw it as hard as you can," he said, popping his mitt with his fist.

"Yes sir," I replied.

As soon as he got back down into his stance I reared back and blazed a pitch into him that was so fast it knocked him right flat on his back. When he got up, he called another time-out and walked back to the mound.

"Thorpe," he said with a rueful grin, "I asked for it. But from here on in, if you don't mind, I'd prefer you not throw it quite that hard."

By the end of the season, I'd played in forty-four games. Jesse and Joe had only stayed on into the late summer, but I stuck it out through September. I won nine, lost ten, and my batting average was .253. It wasn't impressive, but then neither was our league. At the end of the season no less than three of the seven teams claimed they had won the pennant. With all the uproar about final standings, doctored balls, and fixed games, the president of the league resigned.

"The Eastern Carolina League is a laughingstock," he told reporters.

Still, what with the good press I'd gotten in the papers, especially about my fast baserunning, I thought I might stand a chance to move on to the next level. There were rumors that big-league scouts wanted to sign me. But that didn't happen. I was out of work.

Joe Libby went back to Carlisle, where he became captain of the 1909 football team and told Pop about what we'd done down in east Carolina. Me, though, I went home again to Oklahoma. I missed being among family. Mary needed help on her farm and I knew I was the best one to do it.

In October of 1909 I wrote a letter to Carlisle, asking Superintendent Friedman to transfer the money from my account, since I had left school for good. I wanted to get a horse and buggy to use on my sister's farm. His response was that I was supposed to be back at school and that I was a deserter. When students deserted, all funds to their credit were held until they returned.

"Sending you these funds would be bad for discipline," he wrote.

However, he did return the two allotment checks that had arrived at the school after I left. With what little I'd saved up from summer ball and those checks, I went out and bought a horse and buggy and eighty-eight dollars worth of corn and hay to get us through the winter feeding time.

BEING MISSED

Even though I was in Oklahoma, I still followed the fortunes of Carlisle's football team through the 1909 season. It was easy enough to do. Carlisle's football was so well-known that it was covered in just about every paper in America that had any kind of circulation.

The news was not good, however. It had been four years since the University of Pennsylvania came even close to beating Carlisle, but that fall the Indians lost to them by a score of 26–9. The story was pretty much the same when they played Brown. Carlisle could barely get on the board. Then they got beat by Penn State.

Billy Newashe and some of my other friends kept in touch through that disappointing season.

"Jim," Billy wrote to me, "the coaches here miss you very much."

But I stayed on in Oklahoma. Still, even though I had no intention of going back to being a Carlisle boy, I felt bad about that season. The last game was scheduled for Thanksgiving Day in Cincinnati, Ohio, against the University of St. Louis. Pop Warner sent me a letter, along with a train ticket, inviting me to come to that game as his guest. He had always treated me fair and I figured it was the least I could do. I also knew that this game was a real special one for Pop. The coach of the St. Louis team was none other than Pop's own brother, Bill Warner. I packed my valise, got on that train, and went to Cincinnati.

Pop brought me in to talk with the team before the game.

"You're the Carlisle Indians," I said to them. "That means something. I would like to see you go out there today and show them what Indians can do."

It might have done some good, because I saw one whale of a game that day as I sat in the stands. It was the best that Carlisle played all that year. Our team had 161 yards passing and 417 yards running the ball and the final score was 32–0!

I stayed on to have Thanksgiving dinner with the team. Everybody was excited as all get out.

"You come back next fall, Jim," Joe Libby said. "Then nobody will beat us."

I didn't answer him. Even though I'd found myself wishing I was in that game along with my friends, I was far from ready to go back to school.

Since Pop had invited me to his game, I figured I should return the favor. I knew how much he loved the outdoors and it was getting into the shooting season.

"Want to come on out to Oklahoma with me?" I asked him. "There's a few game birds out there with your name on them."

Pop agreed and the two of us went hunting together in Oklahoma. We had a grand time bagging doves and turkeys and then going on for deer. Some of what we took Mary cooked up in fine meals that Pop shared with us. But most of what Pop shot he left at Mary's, knowing that it would help feed the Thorpe clan in the weeks to come.

Much of the time when you hunt, if you are a hunter worth your salt, you don't talk. You have to keep your eyes and ears open, not your mouth. Pop was a fine hunter and understood that. But we did some talking, too, mostly at the end of each day.

"How did your season in the Eastern Carolina Association go?" Pop asked me one evening.

Nothing ever got past Pop when it came to what his athletic boys did, either on the field or off it. I knew that he had quizzed Joe Libby about our time in North Carolina. But he hadn't heard it from me yet. So I told him all about my time at Rocky Mount, from my success at pitching and running the bases to the screwy way the season ended and how I'd been disappointed when no major-league scouts made me an offer.

When I was done, Pop kept quiet for quite a while. He leaned back against a tree stump and worked at rubbing a smudge off the stock of his rifle.

"You know, Jim," he finally said, "you could make more of a name for yourself if you came back to Carlisle. People were just starting to take notice of you on the gridiron. You could be a first-team All-

American for the next two years. And you would be dominant in track and field. You were made to go to the Olympics. Summer ball is fine for those boys who don't have your talent, but Carlisle is where you need to be."

He had a point. I said I would give it some thought.

"Promise me you'll come back to Carlisle," Pop Warner said.

I looked at Pop and knew I couldn't say no. "You'll see me back at Carlisle by Christmas," I promised.

And I kept my word, but not the way Pop expected. Before Christmas I did come back to Carlisle, but it was just to accompany some Sac and Fox boys and girls. I stuck around for the big Christmas party in the gym, where the man in the red suit handing out presents to the little kids may have looked like Santa Claus but was really Pop Warner. I was there for the exchange of presents and the big turkey dinner in the dining hall. But I wasn't there to stay. I spent the holidays there in Pennsylvania with my friends and then took the train back home.

Once again, though, Pop Warner pushed me to return. "Jim," he said, as he saw me off at the depot, "do you promise to come back in the spring?"

This time I didn't say a thing other than good-bye. And when spring rolled around, I headed south to the tobacco towns for another season of pitching in the Eastern Carolina League.

TOUGH SEASONS

Pitching, it turns out, didn't go so well for me that year. I arrived at Cumberland Depot on May 1 of 1910 and had my first practice the very next day. Rather than warming up like I should, I just started right out whipping fast balls to the catcher. By the end of that day, my shoulder hurt some, but I didn't pay it no never mind. The next day it was twinging a little, but I figured the stiffness would work itself out. Turned out, though, that it didn't. My arm was hurt and it didn't get much better that whole season—if ever.

I played twenty-nine games for Rocky Mount that spring and what I did best was run the bases. Nobody was faster in the whole league and nobody was better at stealing bases. If I could just get to first, I was pretty well set. I could steal second and before the pitcher could get the ball to the shortstop or the baseman I was already on my way to third.

"There goes Thorpe," people would yell from the stands.

"Where?"

"Too late, he's already crossed home plate!"

My batting average was only .236 for those twenty-nine games, but I earned my fifteen dollars a week, which was more than the rest of the team could say.

By July 23, well before the official end of the season, the Rocky Mount management figured they'd had enough. Rocky Mount had lost so many games that attendance had dropped way off. The team was disbanded.

Three weeks later, though, I found myself in Fayetteville, eighty miles farther south down the line from Rocky Mount. The team manager, Charley Clancy, liked my baserunning and hired me onto his squad starting August 12. My running was even better there and my batting average started to pick up. I was .253 for the sixteen games I played. Charley was pleased about having me on his nine. He also enjoyed the outdoors about as much as I did, and the two of us went hunting together a time or two.

Before one of those hunting trips, he called the team together. "I've got a photographer here, boys," he said. "I want to get one of you all."

So they took that team picture with me in my Fayetteville Highlanders baseball uniform right in the middle, posing with the rest of the team. Charley really liked that photo. He hung it up on the wall of his office and later on, after I got my little bit of fame, he would point it out to anyone who visited him.

That season ended for me pretty much on the same kind of note it started. I was stealing second. The shortstop was out of place and the second baseman hadn't even seen me coming yet. I'm not saying the pitcher did it on purpose, but when he threw the ball it was hard and straight at my head. I got to second, but my scalp had been torn so badly that I was just gushing blood. I shook my head, sat down on second base, and laughed. What else could I do? I spent the next two days in the hospital and then headed home to Oklahoma.

And that was where I stayed through the rest of that summer and fall and on into the spring of 1911. It wasn't a waste of time. I worked the farm with my sister, went hunting with my relatives and friends, and caught some of the biggest fish I ever caught. When spring rolled around, I decided to play ball again, but I wasn't about to leave home this time. The nearby town of Anadarko was starting up a team, so new that it didn't even have a name, and I was asked if I'd like to pitch for them.

"Sure," I said. "Why not?"

The team owners got a schedule together for us and before long we were playing teams from other leagues as far away as Chicago and Kansas City. The whole first half of the season, we went undefeated and actually had earned the right to the name we finally found for ourselves—the Anadarko Champions. We were called an amateur team, but every one of us got paid a little something, though it was sure not much, even by the standards of the Carolina league. To be honest, the level of ball we were playing was below the Carolina league, too. The Rocky Mount Railroaders had played Class D ball. Anadarko was a few letters farther down the alphabet and the fields we played on were sort of rough-and-tumble. By July, though, we were getting as many as a thousand spectators for each game we played. They had to build more seats in the little plank bleachers.

The final record for the Anadarko Champions that season was 45 wins and only 3 losses, and we tied for the amateur championship of the state. That was about the only statistic that was kept, so I can't really say what my batting average was and I've forgotten how many games I pitched and won, even with my sore arm. I guess part of that was because of the way I parted company with the team.

In mid-July I got called to the manager's office.

"Jim," he said, not looking me in the eye, "we have to let you go. You're too expensive and we've found a cheaper man to take your place."

If that had happened at the start of the season, I think I would have felt bad about being fired for no good reason. But I had an ace up my sleeve now and the manager's words didn't bother me one bit.

I just smiled at him. "Okay," I said. "But you are going to be paying a nickel to read about me sometime soon."

What was that ace up my sleeve? I guess I should say "who." It was none other than my old friend and coach Albert Exendine—Ex. Being a Delaware, Ex was from Anadarko, and I had bumped into him earlier that summer on the main street of town. I can't say that it was an accident. In those days Anadarko was just about big enough to swing a cat in. Everybody knew each other by name and, as a member of our local baseball team, I was enjoying my little share of fame and fans. I'm pretty sure Ex planned that so-called chance meeting of ours. I'm also pretty darn sure that Pop Warner was behind it.

"Why, you've done some growing, Jim," Ex said after we'd greeted each other and pounded each other on the back.

"You could say that," I answered. I was no longer the skinny 165-pounder I'd been during the 1908 football season. I was now close to six foot in height and weighed over 185 pounds without an ounce of fat on me.

"You look like you've kept in pretty decent shape for a little Sac and Fox boy," Ex added, teasing me.

"Good enough to throw any old Delaware I meet," I said, pretending to wrestle with my old friend. Seeing him had put the biggest grin on my face in two years.

"Pop has put together quite a team," Ex said. "All he needs is one more good back. You wouldn't happen to know of one, would you?"

I played dumb. "What do you mean?"

So Ex said it straight out. "Why don't you go back and finish at Carlisle?"

"They wouldn't want me there now."

"You bet they would."

It didn't take much convincing. I allowed that I would like to take another try at Carlisle. Stubborn as I am, it had taken this long for Pop's advice to sink in. But the last year and a half had convinced me.

The only real chance I had to get noticed by the big leagues would be by coming back to Carlisle. Ex and I went together to the telegraph and sent a wire to Pop Warner, indicating I was ready to return and play my part again as a Carlisle Indian. When he got that wire from us, I guess it made his day.

I found out later that Pop went straight to the office of the superintendent.

"Jim Thorpe is ready to return this fall as a student," Pop announced. But Superintendent Friedman was none too pleased at the thought of this prodigal son returning. You see, I had been sort of a thorn in his side over the last two years. I had written one letter after another, both to him and to my Indian agent. I wanted Carlisle to send me back the money of mine they'd held in my savings account at the school.

Superintendent Friedman hated giving up anyone's money. In fact, there had been a sort of scandal at Carlisle in 1910. An audit of the superintendent's books found that he had no fewer than 134 phantom students, boys and girls who'd left school or died or never attended in the first place. That hadn't stopped the superintendent from collecting their government checks to the tune of over thirty-four thousand dollars! He had survived that scandal by paying back the money to the government, but there would be more scandals to come in the future, ones that would finally bring the whole school down.

Maybe that was one of the reasons why Super-intendent Friedman had finally given in to me. In

December of 1910 he had sent me the entire $197.34 that was in my savings account. That had given me enough to make sure all my relatives had a good Christmas and also enough feed to get through the winter. Hearing my name again hadn't put a smile on his face.

"Are you sure we want that boy back here?" he said to Pop Warner. "I have taken the formality of closing out his records."

"Then open 'em up again," Pop said. "Jim Thorpe is going to play football for Carlisle this September."

And Superintendent Friedman knew the subject was closed.

A FRIEND FOR LIFE

When I arrived back at Carlisle, I didn't even bother to stow my bag at the dorm. I went straight to Pop Warner's house. He was sitting on the front steps, holding up and admiring a new eagle feather headdress that he'd just bought. As I've already mentioned, Pop loved Indian art and collected it with a vengeance. He'd later pose with that headdress in full Indian regalia. But when he saw me coming, he put the headdress down, hopped off the steps, grabbed me by both shoulders, and looked me up and down the same way he'd been admiring that war bonnet. Just like Ex had done, he was taking note of the fact that I'd gotten my growth.

"Where have you been?" he said.

Now that was a question he didn't have to ask. I knew full well that Pop had been keeping tabs on me over the last two years. But I answered anyway.

"Playing baseball," I said.

Pop nodded. "Well, son, you won't be doing that here at Carlisle."

I nodded back to him. "Nossir," I agreed. "It's the gridiron for me."

That term, the gridiron, is still used to refer to the football playing field. It came about because of the rules that used to govern where you could throw the ball during passing plays. The field was marked like a big checkerboard with lines drawn not just across the field, but from one end zone to the other, marking it out in a big grid so it looked like one of those grated metal frames used to cook food over a fire. The first two years I played football at Carlisle was on a field with that kind of crisscrossing lines.

Pop shook his head. "It's a gridiron no more, Jim. Take a look at Indian Field. This year it is going to be a whole new game."

Pop was not just flapping his jaws. Good old Indian Field, where I'd spent so many hours, sure did look different. Now the only lines on the field were the yard markers from one side to the other. Once again, there had been big changes made in the rules of football. Your quarterback no longer had to get out of the box, moving five yards to the right or the left of the center, before he could throw. For the first time, too, the length of a game of football had been standardized. We now played four quarters of fifteen minutes each. Scoring, too, was different than it had been when last I played. A field goal was now worth only three points.

Some changes hadn't yet been made, though. A touchdown was still five points, with the extra point for the kick making it six. The length of the field was still 110 yards and when you got the ball you only had three downs, not four. When you punted, it was a free ball. You could sprint downfield, catch your own punt or grab it off the ground, and then run with it.

One new rule that Pop was none too fond of restricted passing. That year of 1911, passes over twenty yards were outlawed, which meant big changes for our game, where throwing the ball forty and fifty yards through the air had been standard. That rule had been put in because of the way the Carlisle Indians played, beating big Ivy League schools with our wide-open passing attack. That passing restriction only lasted a year. Maybe it was because they saw it didn't slow down our Carlisle team.

What a team it was that year! My old friend Sampson Burd, the team captain, was at right end. The other end was Henry Roberts. I knew Henry from back when we were two little kids at Haskell playing with a football made out of rags. Henry, who was Pawnee and from Oklahoma, had been working for the Indian Service in South Dakota until the previous year when Pop got wind of his football talents and brought him to Carlisle. The tackles were Lone Star Dietz and my old Sac and Fox buddy Billy Newashe. The guards were Peter Jordan, who was a Chippewa and worked with me in the tailor shop, and Elmer Busch, who was Pomo from way out in California. Joe Bergie was at center, alternating with Joe Garlow, who went in at guard as well. Joe Garlow was a Tuscarora from New York and the smartest guy on our team when it came to book learning. He just loved to study, but was tough as rawhide on the field. Alex Arcasa, a Colville from way up in Washington State, played right wingback. The other two backs were Possum Powell and me. That was most of our starting lineup and we all played both ways. Our whole team that year never numbered more than seventeen men.

There's one more important player I haven't mentioned. Gus Welch. Our quarterback. He was a great quarterback, probably the second-best Carlisle ever had—right behind Frank Mt. Pleasant. He was a lot like Frank in that he wasn't real big, just five feet nine inches and 155 pounds, but he made up for his size with his thinking and his quick feet. As Pop always put it, the quarterback was the key. I can still hear the words Pop was always repeating about those small quarterbacks of his.

"The battle is not always to the strong, but to the active, the vigilant and the brave," Pop would say. "And the quarterback must be the most active and vigilant of all."

Pop had just published a football primer and was using that big mailing list of his to sell it to just about every college and high school coach in the country. In it he wrote that "the quarterback position is without question the most important on the team." You had to be careful choosing the man for that position because a good quarterback had to be "the liveliest, coolest and headiest player among the candidates." That truly described my friend Gus. My friend, for sure. My best friend. Good old Gus stood by my side in more ways than one.

When I first met Gus, he couldn't speak much

English, and I had no idea how important he'd be in my life. It was at that Minnesota game on November 16 of 1907 in Minneapolis, the one we won 12–10. Sitting on the bench with us was this skinny little half-Chippewa, half-Irish kid. His father had been a logger who died in an accident, and his mom had passed away not long after that from tuberculosis. He and his little brother had been raised by their Chippewa grandparents, in the old way. He'd grown up hunting and fishing, harvesting wild rice and maple sugar. He hadn't even gone to the government Indian school.

But somehow Gus heard about the Carlisle Indians playing in Minnesota. Even though only fifteen, he had made up his mind he wanted to play football. So he went out and trapped a wolf, sold its hide, and used the money to buy a train ticket to Minneapolis. He'd never been in a big city before, but he made his way to the hotel where we were staying before the game. Two of our players were Chippewas, and Gus got them to take him to Pop Warner and translate for him.

Pop was impressed with Gus, small as he was. So he let him sit on the bench with us and encouraged him to apply for admission to Carlisle. A year later, in September of 1908, Gus was on another train, heading east for Pennsylvania with his little brother Jimmy. It turned out that Jimmy didn't like Carlisle at all and went back home to Wisconsin. But Gus did fine. He picked up English as easy as picking up a football, and became a star student and even a member of the debating team. He was quite a storyteller, too. One of my favorites was the one he told about that train trip to Pennsylvania.

"Jimmy and I had never seen a sleeper car before," he said. "So that night as people were getting into their berths, I asked the conductor about it. 'Do we sleep here?' I asked him.

"'Do you have a reservation?' the conductor said.

"'No sir,' I replied. 'We live with my grand-mother.'"

Gus and I ended up roommates. That worked out great. I helped him during practices and, being sharp at academics, he helped me with my studies. Gus was also a better talker. I always tended to say as little as possible, but Gus was never at a loss for words. That helped me when we got into social situations, including those involving the fairer sex. While I stood there tongue-tied, Gus would break the ice with a joke and get everyone laughing. He would do just about anything to help me. Whether we were on the field of play or off it, I knew that Gus Welch always had my back. I had found a loyal friend for life.

30

SO FAR, SO GOOD

"YOU GOLDANG BONEHEAD!" a familiar voice shouted. "GET OVER HERE!"

Even though I knew I was about to get it, it almost made me smile. It had been over two years since I'd heard Pop Warner ball me out for failing to do something to his satisfaction. Pop's practices, which were long and exacting, were never quiet. Before Pop came to Carlisle, from what folks told me, his language on the practice field had been even more colorful. But after his Indian players had gotten together to ask him to please stop swearing at them so much because that wasn't right, Pop had taken their words to heart. It was well known that the Carlisle Indians was hard-nosed, but they were also real gentlemen, including during the games themselves. On more than one occasion, our Carlisle captains would ask the referees to speak to the players on the opposing teams about their use of profanity.

Still, despite his best efforts, Pop's language would get a little blue every now and then when he was excited.

"Ding-dong it, Thorpe. You gotta hit that man, understand? This isn't baseball! This is football!

Here, let me show you how it's done!"

WHOMP! A beefy shoulder came slamming into my midsection, knocking me off my feet.

Pop Warner may have been pushing forty in 1911, but it didn't stop him from pushing his players around like we were tackling dummies. And it was still true that whenever Pop Warner demonstrated a block or a tackle, you went down and stayed there for a while.

Pop yanked me to my feet and patted me on the shoulder. "Got it, Jim?" he said, his voice less excited now. "Let's do it again."

I was working hard to get everything right. I know that there are some who believe what a few of the stories said about me. In those newspaper articles they claimed I just lazed my way through without making any effort. That was far from the truth. Maybe I didn't leap up and dash back to the huddle like some of those Ivy League ballcarriers did after they got tackled. But that was just because I didn't want to waste any of the energy I'd need once the play really started. I didn't get better just because of natural ability but from doing the same plays over and over again until I had them learned perfectly. Practice really does make perfect.

Part of the reason why people got the impression that all I had was natural ability was because Pop encouraged that kind of picture. Making me out to be some kind of superhuman savage made me scarier to our opponents. Just in case anyone ever forgot I was an Indian, Pop's publicity machine was there to remind them of it.

But whatever was written about me and the Carlisle team that year, when our season opener came I was raring to go. Billy Newashe wasn't back yet from Oklahoma and so we didn't have our whole first team, but I figured we would do just fine against Lebanon Valley. Gus Welch, though, was suffering from the jitters. This was going to be his first game at quarterback. It was the quarterback's job to block the end on Play # 48—the first he was planning to call, starting with a pitch to me at wingback.

"What do I do if I miss the end on forty-eight?" Gus asked me.

"Keep going," I said.

Sure enough, when Gus went to block that end, the man stepped aside. Gus lowered his head and took aim at the halfback and missed him, too. Next in line was the safety, who moved out of Gus's way like he was avoiding a freight train!

"What do I do now, Jim?" Gus yelled, looking back at me over his shoulder, where I had been running behind him all the time as we went down the field.

"Nothing," I said, handing the ball to the referee in the end zone. "We just scored a touchdown."

After that, Gus lost his jitters. The score ended up 53–0 and it could have been twice that.

Four days later, Muhlenberg College was the next to hit the Carlisle Field—and land on their backsides. Muhlenberg was a small Lutheran school and they had brought a small squad—only sixteen players. When they got out of the horse-drawn hack that had brought them from the rail station, they looked like condemned men. They were taken on a tour of the gym before the game and they walked in hushed silence past the team photos of our squad and the rows of trophies won in past years. By the time the game started, they were already whipped. The first time I tore through their line, they just bounced off me. I looked back after crossing the goal line and half their team was on the ground, groaning. It was 32–0 by the half and we took pity on those poor boys after that.

Our third warm-up game was another story. We were going against Dickinson College. As I've mentioned before, a good many of our students went to Dickinson for advanced courses. We were no strangers to them, and as a result, they weren't as afraid of us big bad Indians as some were. Not only that, their quarterback that year, Hyman Goldstein, was like a little bulldog. He was hard to catch when he had the ball and the first one to hit you when it came your way. He may have weighed only 165 pounds, but he went for my legs and took me down all by himself more than once. Neither team scored in the first half. We eventually wore them down, though I broke free for an eighty-five-yard touchdown run and we won the game 17–0. It had been no easy match and both sides felt good about the game.

From then on in, Pop invited Dickinson College to be

our regular opponents for our Wednesday scrimmages. Some of those Wednesday practice games turned into wars and I have no doubt that some of the success we had that season was because those battles against the boys from the other end of town made us sharper.

Next came Mount St. Mary's. I scored three touchdowns in the first half before letting our other backs take a turn—46–5 was the final tally. That was the end of the soft part of our schedule. It had been years since Carlisle had lost a game on Indian Field. Road games were always a bigger challenge and now we were about to travel to Washington, DC, for the Georgetown game.

Gus Welch went down ahead of us along with Pop's head scout, Cap Craver, to watch the Georgetown practices. Back then, Carlisle was just about the only team in the country to send scouts to watch the other team and figure out their plays before the actual game.

What Gus and Cap saw was put to good use in our strategy. Our first score came after only seven minutes. Then I made a forty-five-yard run that set up a touchdown by Possum, with me kicking the extra point. I tackled the Georgetown ballcarriers for a loss twice and then the ball was ours again. I faked a punt and made another long run to set up Possum's second touchdown. Aside from kicking, I didn't score that day, but I felt fine about what I did.

Some of the stories in the press were typical of the stuff they always wrote about Carlisle.

Not since Custer made his last stand against Sitting Bull at the Little Big Horn has a battle between redskins and palefaces been so ferociously fought as that which was waged on Georgetown Field.

It was a lot better when they just talked about the game, even though they still tended to exaggerate my part. I never let that kind of press go to my head, though. I knew that I was only as good as my team and I kept working hard with Gus, helping him out on the field like he was helping me in my classes. By October Gus was heading for the Carlisle Honor Roll and I was getting good grades in all my classwork.

Best of all, we were undefeated on the field. So far, so good, I thought. But there were five games to go and I knew they would be the toughest ones of all.

IVA

October 21. We got off the train in Pittsburgh. We knew that we had to play a tougher team than any of those we had played thus far. Pittsburgh would be no pushover. But, to be honest, I was looking ahead two weekends. And it wasn't just because that was when we'd play our first Ivy League rival, the University of Pennsylvania. It was also because of Iva.

Iva Margaret Miller was the prettiest girl at Carlisle. Everyone agreed about that. Especially me. When she first showed up in September of 1911, everybody took notice. I didn't say a word to her then. But even though I might have been tongue-tied, I wasn't blind. More than one of us Indian boys took a shine to her. Had it been just a year earlier, I would not have stood a snowball's chance in July. However, by the time late October rolled around, I had a few arrows in my quiver.

One of them was that I now had about the biggest name on campus. Being a football star meant a lot of things and one of them was that a girl like Iva—who was not just beautiful and graceful and athletic, but also as smart as a whip—would give me a second glance.

Another thing in my favor was my friend Sampson Burd.

"There's one girl I would not mind escorting," Sam said as we watched Iva pass one day on campus, both of us being careful not to stare.

"Me, too," I said, surprising myself as much as I did Sam. I'd never paid that much attention to the ladies before. Of course, in recent years, there hadn't been such things as dances where Indian boys and girls could get together. But by 1911 the social rules had loosened up enough so that such events—well chaperoned to be sure—were now possible.

"Why, Jim," Sam said, "I believe you are smitten."

From that point on, my good buddy Sam, who was one of the best talkers on campus, became my go-between.

Every year there was at least one big game where a considerable number of the young women of Carlisle would be allowed to attend. Sam introduced me to Iva, and then, when I was not able to do more than mumble, he added that I would appreciate the opportunity to invite her to attend the game at the University of Pennsylvania as my guest and to escort her to the big dance on that weekend. To my surprise and everlasting delight, she accepted.

But first we had to dispose of Pittsburgh and Lafayette. At Pitt, my kicking game was at its best. I was always able to punt the ball farther than most—sixty or seventy yards. I also put those punts up so high that I could get downfield under them before anyone else. Because a punt was a free ball, you were allowed to catch your own kick and advance it. I did that twice, once for a touchdown. We won that game 17–0 and the story in the *Pittsburgh Dispatch* made me feel proud when I read such words as these:

> *This person Thorpe was a host in himself. Tall and sinewy, as quick as a flash and as powerful as a turbine engine, he appeared to be impervious to injury. Kicking from 50 to 70 yards every time his foot crashed against the ball, he seemed possessed of superhuman speed, for wherever the pigskin alighted, there he was, ready to grab it or to down the Pitt player who secured it. At line-bucking and general all-around work, this Sac and Fox shone resplendent and then some.*

To be sure, that story, which went into my scrap-book, earned me some teasing from the other football boys.

"How's your engine, Jim?" Billy Newashe and the other linemen would ask when they gang-tackled me in practice. "Getting low on oil yet?"

Or Alex Arcasa might poke me with a pencil in class. If I said "Ow," he'd crack back, "But I thought you were impervious to injury."

I wish I really had been impervious to injury the next weekend when we traveled to Easton for the Lafayette game. It was another shutout for us, 19–0 and the first three quarters went fine for me. I scored a touchdown, kicked an extra point and a field goal.

But in the final quarter I twisted my ankle so badly I could not stand up on it. They had to carry me out of the game. And that Penn game was the next weekend!

November 4. I was pretty glum when I gingerly climbed on board the horse-drawn bus that took us from Carlisle to the train station at Gettysburg Junction. I was going to suit up, but I really hadn't been able to practice that week. I wasn't even able to kick. Even the crowd of students cheering us out through the gate of the school didn't lighten my mood.

Strangely enough, it was Mr. Pope who managed to make me feel better. Mr. Pope, who was the bus driver, always moved with a kind of quiet dignity. It made me wonder if maybe one of his great-grandpas back in the days before slavery had been a chief and some of that had come down to him. We both knew what it was like to live in a different world than the one our ancestors had known, a world where we were judged by our skin. I always made it a point to say hello and good-bye when he drove us places—something Pop Warner usually failed to do.

I was the last one to limp off at the station, and Mr. Pope held up a hand as I started to pass by him.

"Mr. Jim," he said, "you do what you can and accept what you can't."

"Yes sir," I said.

So, despite the fact that Iva Miller was there in the

stands and yet I was not going to be able to play, I made the best of things. I cheered my team on and encouraged them to do their best.

And that was what they did. Pop had been scheming all week at ways to bamboozle Penn, and he did so on our first scoring play. Lone Star Dietz dropped back from tackle to become a ballcarrier, took the handoff from Gus, and ran straight down the middle for a touchdown. As he crossed the line, he leaned over without breaking stride to touch the ball to the grass and then hold it high over his head. Our little Carlisle cheering section in the stands of Franklin Field went wild, and I yelled louder than any of them from my front-row seat on the bench.

On the first Penn pass Possum intercepted the ball. Then Gus called his own number and zigzagged down the field with Penn players bouncing off him for an eighty-five-yard touchdown.

It was another Carlisle shutout. Penn lost 16–0 and I was able to go to that dance with a contented mind because my teammates had played their hearts out and my being injured had not cost us a victory.

I was so happy that I almost ruined my whole evening with one offhand remark. We all went out to dinner that night at the Normandie Hotel in Philadelphia, where we always stayed when we played Penn. By all of us I mean just that. It wasn't just our starting squad. As a special treat, Pop's secretary, Mr. Martin, had brought the two dozen scrub players on our team to watch the game. They'd been treated to a free lunch at Gimbel's Department Store and had been entertained by the Carlisle girls, who sang school songs and did recitations. Iva Miller was featured in that performance. She'd been put forward as an outstanding entertainer ever since her early days as a little girl at Chilocco Indian School in Oklahoma.

Of course, those Carlisle girls were included as special guests at our dinner, each of us accompanying our own date—under the watchful eagle eyes of such married lady chaperones as Pop's wife. No girl's reputation would be ruined by being allowed to be alone for a moment with a young man.

As soon as I saw Iva, a big goofy grin just spread over my face and I blurted out the first thing that came into my head.

"You're a cute little thing," I said.

The look she gave me told me that she was considering making her way to the nearest exit. I was never a sharp dresser—in fact Iva later told me that her first thought when she saw me was that I didn't care much about my appearance. Now, to top it off, I had started off the evening by acting like a clodpoll.

Before long, though, I had managed to redeem myself some. I might never have been a ladies' man, but I surprised her when I invited her up to the dance floor. For that was the third arrow in my quiver. I had been learning how to ballroom dance. I approached it like it was another sport and eventually would get so good at it that I would win prizes. Iva held her hand out, and when I took it, I felt like a hundred volts of electricity had just shot through me. Despite the fact that my ankle was killing me, we did a two-step together that was the best on the floor that night.

As we talked, I learned more about Iva, including why her hair and skin were fairer than most at Carlisle. Despite the fact that she had gone to Indian schools all her life, the most Indian ancestry she had in her was just a trace of Cherokee from her mother's side. Her mother had died when Iva was only four, and her father, who ran a hotel in Okmulgee, Oklahoma, had decided that the only way to get an education for her was in the Indian school system. So he managed to wangle her way into Chilocco when she was eight.

Being so fair-skinned had made it hard for her at times. I understood that, having been called a half-breed myself a time or two. But Iva was as tough as she was pretty, and she had such a way of making friends and treating others good that even being the most beautiful girl at Carlisle didn't earn her any enemies.

By the end of that evening at the Normandie, Iva and I were as thick as thieves. She favored me with a sweet smile as she went upstairs with the other young ladies and their chaperones.

Someday, when I'm a success, I said to myself, I am going to make her Iva Margaret Thorpe.

HARVARD

If any contest of that 1911 season was the biggest, it was the one against Harvard. That game was one of the two greatest I ever played. (The second one was against West Point the next season.) My ankle was still sprained. The week before we played the Harvard Crimson, Pop had tried everything on it, including things that wouldn't become standard practice in sports for another two or three decades. He didn't just use liniment, but massage, vibrating machines, and even electricity. It helped some, but I was supposed to give it at least another week to heal. However, I wasn't about to stay out and Coach Warner agreed.

"Tape," he said. "That's the ticket." He cased my ankle in adhesive plaster and then taped me from my toes all the way up to my knee. My leg looked like it belonged to an Egyptian mummy. It was so tight that it creaked when I walked. But it did the trick.

Only sixteen of our players made that trip to the Crimson oval, the biggest concrete stadium in the entire world. I never saw anything close to it until I traveled in Europe and visited the Roman Colosseum. Harvard Stadium was packed with forty thousand people that day, just about all of them Harvard fans chanting "Kill the Indians."

That might have daunted some teams, I'm sure. Harvard was regarded as one of the best teams in America that year. They had only given up fourteen points in six games that year. The fifty varsity players who made up three full squads of the Crimson not only outnumbered us, they were physically bigger as well. Even their second team was supposed to be the match of any in the country, and that was what Harvard started against us.

Their coach, Mr. Percy Haughton, didn't much like Pop and looked down his nose at our little team. As far as he was concerned his big challenges were yet to come against Yale and Dartmouth and Brown. In fact, he didn't even go to the game. He went off to New Haven to scout Yale, leaving his assistant coaches in charge and telling them to rest his best first-team players who'd racked up some injuries when they'd played Princeton.

I was a little stiff and unsteady on my feet when the game started, but I got warmed up fast. I was used as a decoy and a blocker at first, with the ball going to Possum straight down the middle. That took us most of the way down the field, but we couldn't score and gave the ball up to Harvard. They had plenty of players to use as substitutes while we played the same eleven or twelve men the whole game. And despite all this advantage, Harvard couldn't get it across our goal.

On our second possession, Gus, whose ballhandling was great that day, started using the reverse. He handed off to Alex, who ran to the outside and handed the ball to me running in the opposite direction. With Sam Burd and Pete Jordan ahead of me as blockers, I started picking up big yards. Once again, we stalled short of the Harvard end zone, but this time I kicked a thirteen-yard field goal. Harvard answered with one of their own. Then I kicked a forty-three-yarder putting us back ahead 6–3. Before the half ended, the ball got loose on an exchange between Alex and Gus, and Harvard took it in for a touchdown.

We went in to the locker room trailing by a score of 9–6, but none of us were discouraged. We knew we were outplaying those bigger, stronger Harvard boys.

I was a marked man when the second half began.

"Get Thorpe. Get Thorpe!" was the chant from the stands. Even when I didn't have the ball I usually ended up surrounded by a sea of potential red-jerseyed tacklers.

"How's the ankle holding up, Jim?" Coach Warner asked.

All I said was "Fine." The ankle hurt like blazes and talking about it would have just made it worse when I still had two full quarters to play. In fact, the only other talking I did during the first three periods of that game was to one of the referees. I don't know if he had dressed that way on purpose, but he was wearing a red sweater and golf trousers that looked almost exactly like a Harvard uniform. I must have dodged him a dozen times in my open field runs, thinking he was about to tackle me. Twice I ended up running right into the arms of a real Harvard player.

"Sir," I asked him, "could you please change your sweater?" But I guess he forgot to do it.

In the third quarter I kicked another field goal and made a long run that set up the ball close to the end zone. We faked the reverse and Alex carried it across. Now we were ahead 15–9 and those Harvard boys was worried. Bob Fisher, who was their team captain, and their All-American halfback Percy Wendell had seen enough. They were not about to follow Coach Haughton's plan of holding them out for Yale any further. The last thing they wanted was a loss to lowly Carlisle.

"We're going in," Fisher said to Assistant Coach Perry at the end of the third quarter.

A roar went up from the stands that shook the stadium as those nine star Harvard players in clean red jerseys came lumbering onto the field.

"Give me the ball," I said to Gus Welch. "And get out of my way. I mean to do some real running."

Those fresh new men on the Harvard side managed to make a difference for a while. They burst through our worn-out blockers and stopped our reverses. But I just began to run up the middle. I'd bounce off one tackler, run over another, and carry the third one another five yards before going down. Those was some of the toughest yards I ever ran and my ankle was getting sorer every minute, but I didn't stop. Pop tried to take me out of the game, but I shook my head and held on to the ball as we held on to the lead. We gained 334 yards that day, and 173 of them was from my running.

But we were getting weaker. We knew that Harvard was almost certain to score before the game ended. We needed more points. We had the ball on the Crimson forty-eight and it was third down. Remember, we only had three downs then, not four. We could either try to make a first, fail and give it up on downs, or punt. But Gus had another idea.

"Field goal," he said.

"Who ever heard of a field goal from here?" I said. "Punt the ball."

"Nope," Gus said. "You're going to make it, Jim."

I took a look in my friend's eyes and knew I had to try. I stepped back a couple of extra paces and waited for the snap. Bad ankle or not, the game depended on me. When I hit that ball, I hit it solid. The ball was low at first and a Harvard defender got a hand on it, but I had driven it so hard that it just kept going. It went right through the middle of the goal and landed twenty yards behind it. We were ahead 18–9 with only three minutes to go.

Sure enough, Harvard did get that final score. A few plays later when I went to kick, my ankle slowed me. The Harvard center blocked the kick, grabbed it, and took it in for a touchdown. That made it 18–15. But when we got control of the ball again, we refused to give it up. We moved it down the field until the clock ran out at just about the same time my leg did.

They had to carry me off the field, but I didn't care. Even those Harvard fans were cheering for me and our little Indian team. It was one of the best days of my whole life.

ALL-AMERICAN

Back at Carlisle, the whole town went wild with the news of the Harvard victory. People came out in droves to cheer as Carlisle students snake-danced through the town carrying torches in a procession that featured a stretcher with a bandaged dummy on it wearing the Harvard Crimson. Even though our quarterback, Gus Welch, had a wrenched back so sore he couldn't hardly walk and most of our players were so banged up we moved like old men, Pop Warner was grinning along with the rest of us as we went through a light practice that Monday. Talk went around that there was no question now what team was going to be called the national champions that year.

Pride, though, always goes before a fall. On November 18, we traveled to Syracuse for our tenth game of the season. Every week, Pop Warner had told the press that our team was going to let down and lose. He said the same thing that week about Syracuse.

"We are not taking the Orangemen lightly," Pop said. "This contest may bring the end to our winning string."

It had gotten to the point where the news reporters no longer believed him. The general consensus was that the only thing that could stop us from whipping Syracuse was if our train crashed on the way. There was no train wreck, but there might as well have been. What was waiting for us at Archbold Stadium was the worst weather of the year. A howling wind dropped buckets of cold rain all through the game. The field was nothing but freezing slush. To make things worse, Gus Welch's back had not healed enough to suit up and we had to play without our best quarterback.

Despite the weather, eleven thousand spectators were there, most of them chanting "Get Thorpe! Get Thorpe!" I don't remember much of that game, aside from the try for an extra point that skidded off the side of my foot. Even though I did score two touchdowns and make the other extra point, my mistake lost the game for us. Syracuse won by the score of 12–11.

"You kept us in the game, Jim," Sam Burd said to me as we trudged off through the mud while Syracuse celebrated. The other boys and even Pop said much the same. But that didn't console me and it didn't get me to lift up my head. In one week I'd gone from the greatest game I'd ever played to what in my mind was the worst.

Our practices that week were not the light ones we'd had after Harvard. Pop worked us to the bone and we were glad of it. My disappointment turned to determination. As far as I was concerned that was the last time I was going to get beat at anything that year. Gus's back got better and our whole first team was back in shape. We were more than ready when we hit the field against Johns Hopkins on November 22. On our first two series we took the ball the length of the field both times. I was the one carrying the mail and scored both touchdowns. It was so easy that Pop pulled me and most of the rest of the first string out to let some of the boys who hadn't seen much action get into the game. The final score, even with our second string playing, was 26–9.

Then it was November 30. Brown University was the final game of the season and all the newsmen were picking them to beat us. After all, Brown had proven itself able to beat the best of the Ivy Leaguers and we had lost to lowly Syracuse. They had one of the strongest defenses in America and, as was the usual case, they outweighed us at every position. Then there was the weather. That Thanksgiving morning in Providence turned out to be worse than it had been at Syracuse. It was even wetter and colder. And after the first half, the steady rain and wind turned into heavy snow.

But we were not about to be beat. Possum attacked the center of the line and I made long runs around the ends. Lone Star pulled the tackle around end play again and gained yards. A desperation tackle stopped me just short of a score and we gave up the ball on downs, but even though they pushed the ball down the field, they weren't able to make anything out of it.

Our one touchdown came in that first half on a play we'd practiced that week. Instead of a signal count, Gus simply tapped Joe Bergie, our center, and Joe snapped the ball. Gus, whose back was no longer bothering him, took it sixty-two yards around right end. My toe was back up to snuff, too. I had to scrape the mud off my shoe before each kick, but I booted the extra point as well as field goals of twenty-seven and thirty-three yards. My punting, even in that awful weather, was on track, too. My best was an eighty-three-yarder from our own twelve to the Brown fifteen-yard line. We won by the score of 12–6 and felt like we had earned the big Thanksgiving dinner we shared that afternoon back at the hotel.

On the train back to Carlisle, the team voted me in as next year's team captain. And not long after, when Walter Camp named his All-American team, my name was on his list.

All of that made me feel real good, but I didn't have much time to sit back and think about it. Not only did I have to get back into my classes, another season was about to start. I traded my football uniform and cleats for the sneakers, striped knee socks, white shorts, and maroon shirt of the basketball squad. The starting five was myself, Possum, Joel Wheelock, Henry Roberts, and Bruce Goesback.

But that winter wasn't all sports and studies. There was time for the holiday parties and dances. At Christmas, just like every year, Santa Claus showed up in the gym with his big white beard and his red suit and black boots. His laugh seemed a little more booming than usual as Carlisle students came up one by one to get the neatly wrapped presents that were as much a part of the annual social as old Saint Nick himself. The King's Daughters, one of our school social organizations, had been raising the money for those presents all through the year. Pop Warner was always one of those who gave a generous donation.

"Ho ho ho, Merry Christmas!" Santa called. He was in one heck of a good mood, for sure.

Then, as the final gifts were being handed out, someone noticed that Pop Warner, who'd always been Santa before, was standing in the crowd watching the festivities. That was when Gus and Sam and Billy came up to Santa and, even though he protested, pulled off his cap and white beard.

"Look here," Billy yelled, "Santa is an All-American!"

I grinned as the crowd in the gym all cheered me in my Santa suit. Iva Miller, who was to be my partner at the dance later, was right in the front. She was smiling and applauding with everyone else. Not only was I a football hero, the prettiest and smartest young woman I had ever met was my girl. I didn't think there was anyone in the world as lucky as me.

They serenaded me then with the Carlisle school song and I felt a lump in my throat. Carlisle hadn't been an easy place for me during my first years there, so far away from home. I knew that it had been a place to run away from for most of the students who had been brought there against their will during its earlier years. At Carlisle, Indian boys and girls had been mistreated and beaten and made to be ashamed of being Indian. And there was that graveyard out back where none of us ever went if we could avoid it. The names on the markers were of boys and girls who'd been torn away from families that never saw them again.

When I'd left Carlisle three years before I'd never intended to come back again. There were lots of reasons to hate the Carlisle Indian Industrial School. But as I looked around at the faces of my friends, I felt something else. I thought of how proud it made everyone to see us Indians win on the field of battle against the biggest and best schools in America. We were showing the world what Indians could do, that we were just as good as anyone—if not better. Carlisle wasn't just a place, it was also the people who went here, struggled and succeeded against all odds. Dear old Carlisle, I thought, and shook my head as I thought it. I knew then that there was nowhere else in the world I'd ever love and hate as much. No matter how far I traveled.

The last thing they did was call Pop Warner forward. He was holding an American flag that he put into my hands.

"You know where you will carry this, Jim."

I nodded as everyone cheered again. Just like Pop, I was thinking now of the Olympic Games.

34

BETTER THAN EVER BEFORE

"Jim is doing everything he tries better now than ever before in his career."

A dozen newsmen wrote those words down as Pop Warner spoke them. It was March 9, 1912. We were in Pittsburgh for the Pittsburgh Athletic Club Indoor Track Meet and Pop was, as usual, predicting success for me in the five events where I'd be competing.

It always embarrassed me to hear such things said about me. Pop, though, was in his element. I don't think he knew how to be embarrassed. But at least I wasn't the only one he was bragging about now that our indoor track season had begun. Louis Tewanima was still the best distance runner in America and Gus Welch was proving himself to be just as outstanding in the middle-distance races. Gus, in fact, had been chosen as our team captain.

I was no longer playing basketball. Once the track season was in full swing, I had to devote myself to practice. I don't know how many times I jumped over that bar in the gym to land on those hard mats on the other side, but my work was paying off. I was clearing six feet with no trouble at all on every jump. I was also increasing my distance in the shot put. We pounded around the indoor board track and whenever the weather broke, Gus and I were outside on the cinder oval. We ran with Louis there as well, but his runs usually only started on the track because he was getting ready for the marathon. His training took him miles beyond, along the walkways and roads of Carlisle. All through the winter and spring of 1912 Pop kept us busy. We had our eyes on Sweden. The Olympic Games.

Jim throwing the javelin, 1912

I was no longer the shy Indian boy who could hardly put two words together in public. I was giving talks to the younger students, mostly about athletics at Carlisle and the importance of trying their best. My writing was improving, at least according to Miss Marianne Moore. You might know her name. She would go on to become one of the most famous poets in America. Carlisle was her first job, but young as she was, she was a fine teacher. Having her say that about me meant something. Gus and Samson and Iva and I were her favorite students. In fact, Gus and I liked her so well that we had become protective of her. She was a delicate little thing. Her legs only just about reached the pedals on the bicycle she rode to class each day. So us football boys made ourselves available to squire her around when she went into town.

I knew for a fact that she enjoyed the attention and had a good opinion of me. One day, I was waiting for Miss Moore outside the office where she was talking with the superintendent. It was threatening rain and I had appointed myself to hold her umbrella while she pushed her bike. So I just chanced to overhear what she said about me when Mr. Friedman asked how I was doing.

"Jim is still a bit laborious in the classroom," she said, "but he's dependable. Outside the classroom he's modest and casual about everything he has achieved. He is a chivalrous, decent, and cooperative young man."

Those words made my ears burn. They were far too kind, but it did inspire me to try to live up to them. And I had another reason for especially wanting to improve my writing: letters. I knew that if I was fortunate enough to go to the Olympics, I'd want to be able to keep in touch with Iva through letter writing.

From how I did at that Pittsburgh meet, I was right on track to get there. I took first place in the shot put, the running high jump, the sixty-yard dash, and the sixty-yard hurdle, and did much the same at every other indoor meet, taking first or second place in every event I tried. Gus was doing well himself, taking first in the three hundred yards and the other middle-distance races.

May came and the outdoor season got into swing. I kept on winning, but what tickled me the most and got the most publicity for our track squad that spring was actually something that Louis did. The annual Pennsylvania Athletic Association Meet was held that spring in Harrisburg. I wasn't there because the pre-Olympic competition for the pentathlon was being held that same day in New York City. Louis Tewanima agreed to run to Harrisburg all the way from Carlisle as a publicity stunt to draw attention to the Pennsylvania meet. My little Hopi friend covered the eighteen miles in an hour and fifty minutes, arriving just as the two-mile race was starting. Even though he'd done what he set out to do, he joined that race. Some say that he went on and won it, but that wasn't true. Louis just caught up with the pack of runners, passed them, and circled the track twice before calling it a day.

Our last dual meet of the season was against Lafayette. I've heard it told that when Pop Warner got off the train, he was asked where his track team was.

"Right here," he supposedly said, pointing to me, Gus, and Louis.

That is just a story, however. There were actually seven of us who competed that day for Carlisle. I took six first places, Gus won the half mile and the quarter, Samson Burd was first in the hammer throw, and Louis was the winner of the mile and two mile. The final score was 71–41 in favor of Carlisle.

On the basis of how well we'd done throughout that spring, neither Louis nor I had to take part in the Olympic tryouts being held at Harvard. We were named as members of the 164-man Olympic team that would make the trip to Sweden. The only thing that made me sad was that Gus wouldn't be with us. He got sick with some kind of fever that spring, and even though he shook it off over the summer, he was too ill to compete. I'd been making some new friends, though. One of them was Abel Kiviat. I met him in New York at the pentathlon competition and we hit it right off.

"We're both tribal people," he said to me with a grin. "Mine, being Jewish, is that of Abraham."

Abel's specialty was the fifteen hundred meters, where he was the world record holder. Everyone figured he was a shoo-in for the Olympic gold. And he was also pretty good at the other four pentathlon events, the long jump, the javelin, the two hundred, and the discus. He was a big one on technique and did everything just right. The only thing was that, no matter what he did, I did it better.

When I heaved the shot put ten feet farther than he did and won the competition, Abel couldn't take it any longer. He just had to say something.

"Jim, you're doing everything wrong from your footwork to your stance." Then he started laughing. "I don't know how you do it. It's all backward, but you're still beating everybody on the track. You are a marvel."

Abel ended up being my roommate on board the S.S. *Finland*, the ship we took to Sweden.

Louis Tewanima was still having his own successes, too. Pop Warner took us both to a final pre-Olympic meet in New York City on June 12. I beat the U.S. champion high jumper with one of my best heights ever—six feet five inches. Then Pop entered Louis in the thirty-five-hundred-meter run, a distance he'd never tried before, against the two strongest

Louis Tewanima, Pop Warner, and Jim Thorpe, 1912

American runners. Mr. James Edward Sullivan, the head of the Amateur Athletic Union, came up to Pop and asked him what he was doing.

"Why do you run the boy in this event?" he asked.

"He needs the workout," Pop said without batting an eyelash.

Workout or not, Louis beat them all by four yards.

I showed Louis some of the stories that were appearing in the papers about him. "Savage Hopi Indian Transformed into Model Student" was how the headlines usually went. They loved to run the before and after pictures of how Louis and his fellow Hopis looked when they arrived at Carlisle with their long hair and earrings and then in their neat military uniforms.

"What do you think of this?" I said to Louis. "It says that you were a heathen sun worshipper and a crude specimen of a lower order of civilization before you came to Carlisle five years ago, but now you are a member of a Christian congregation."

Louis smiled. "I say I am going to run fast."

Our names were in the paper all the time now and there were more well-wishers than you could shake a stick at. But I soon found out that not everyone was enthusiastic about Indians going to Europe. I needed some money for expenses. So I wrote a letter to Horace Johnson, the new superintendent of our Sac and Fox Agency:

Dear Sir,

Please send me $100 from my account. Will need same this summer in taking trip to Sweden with Olympic team.

Very Respectfully,

James Thorpe

Superintendent Friedman sent a covering note with it, urging that the funds be transferred as soon as possible. But what we got in reply was far from what I'd hoped.

"I have to advise," my Indian agent wrote, "that I cannot conscientiously recommend to the Indian Office that this be done. He is 25 years of age and should be perfectly content to make his own living without depending on trust and lease funds which have cost him no effort to obtain.

"I understand that a trip to Sweden might be of considerable benefit to the young man but I am strongly convinced that instead of being a benefit it will be a determent. He has now reached the age when, instead of gallivanting around the country, he should be at work on his allotment, or in some other location, where, instead of being a tax on his resources, he would be adding something thereto."

When it came to government dealings with Indians, some things never changed.

Finally the day we'd been waiting for arrived. On June 14, 1912, at nine o'clock in the morning, we boarded the S.S. *Finland* in the port of New York City. The gangplank was pulled in, the anchor was pulled up, the big whistle blew, and we steamed out of New York Harbor. We went past the Statue of Liberty and Ellis Island, where immigrants seeking land came in to America. Of course, Louis had seen it all before. He might have been a little Hopi from the mesas of Arizona, but having been to the Olympics in England four years ago, he was an old hand at ocean travel.

Even so, both of us leaned over the rail and looked hard at those two landmarks of a country that hadn't always been kind to us or our ancestors. But any thoughts of hardship were soon overcome by the excitement of where we were bound. We were on our way to the Olympic Games!

OLYMPIC GLORY

"This thing is bigger than most towns in Oklahoma," I said, looking down the long expanse of deck and then peering up at the tall smokestack of the S.S. *Finland*.

That ship we were on was something! I'd been told that I would see some sights I'd never forget in Stockholm, but nothing compared with that huge boat. Boarding it and touring its decks that first day was the biggest thrill of my whole Olympic trip. Imagine taking a big hotel and then setting it afloat. That's what it was like.

On that ship were 164 American boys. (Although there were some women's events, the U.S. Olympic team back then was all-male.) We were the best and biggest Olympic team ever put together by the United States. We weren't all college boys, either. We came from all walks of life. Pat McDonald, our best shot putter who would go on to win the gold, was a New York City cop. We were all colors on board that ship, too. Louis and I weren't even the only Indians. Andrew Sockalexis, who was a marathoner like Louis, was a Penobscot from Maine. Then there was Duke Makoe Hulikohoa Kahanamoku. Duke was the best swimmer in the world and he was a Hawaiian islander.

His ancestors had been the royal family of that island and Duke held his head up just as high as any European prince or king.

There have been stories told about how I never worked a lick during that ten-day voyage. People have said I just laid around in my bunk or stretched out on a deck chair. I guess that is part of the whole myth about how I was just a natural athlete, but I take it as a backhanded compliment. Neither Pop Warner nor our team coach Mike Murphy would have stood for that kind of behavior. Plus I was not going to Sweden to lose. I knew I had to stay in top shape. We had weights set up in the bow of the ship and I lifted them regularly to keep my strength up for the throwing events I'd be doing. Inside we had ropes to vault over to keep us sharp in the high jump, with wrestling mats piled together for us to land on. I ran laps around the deck and did calisthenics every day. Ralph Craig, another of our top-notch runners, was my favorite running partner. We were always pushing each other, doing sprints.

"Jim, we may be overdoing this a bit," Ralph said one day, resting with his hands on his knees and sweat pouring down his brow.

"Want to go again?" I answered.

The only ones who had a hard time training were those who were seasick. One of them, I'm sad to say, was Louis. He couldn't run at all during that whole trip.

He wasn't about to give up, though, even sick as a dog.

"Louis," I heard Pop say to him one day, "win that marathon and you'll have a bankroll big enough to choke a horse."

"You betcher, Pop," Louis replied, his face gray. "I'm going to try hard."

We docked first at Antwerp, Belgium, on June 24 and were given a few days to stretch out at the Beerschot Athletic Club. It was great to run on a surface that wasn't rocking up and down, and I felt like I was in good shape. After that it was another four days to get to Stockholm. The Olympic stadium was close enough to the pier that we could keep on using the S.S. *Finland* as our quarters. So every night we came back to those bunks we had gotten used to during our long journey. Pop also paid for me to make use of a private training ground outside town where I kept on working, getting ready for those five events that make up the pentathlon.

On July 6, 1912, the games opened. Those ceremonies were really something. There were thirty thousand spectators watching from the stands as we came marching in. About twenty-five hundred of us, from twenty-eight different nations, walked in to take our places on the field. I've heard it said that no Olympic Games were ever better organized than that fifth Olympiad, and I think I would have to agree. They called it the "Swedish masterpiece," and it deserved the name. Everything ran like clockwork.

A chorus of more than four thousand started singing the song "A Mighty Fortress Is Our God." I recognized the tune, even though the words were being sung in German. Their voices just filled that big new stadium. As we marched past the royal box, King Gustav of Sweden and Grand Duke Dmitri of Russia doffed their hats and held them over their hearts.

It was the first Olympics where they used an international team of judges to keep things fair. It was also the first time they used loudspeakers and electronic timers. Everything was state of the art.

"All out for the hundred," came the call over the loudspeaker right after the opening ceremony.

Our American team was ready for it. That hundred-meter run was the first event of the game and our boys swept it. They took first, second, and third. That was a shock to the crowds, who had expected at least one or two of the European favorites to take a place.

The next day, Sunday July 7, was the pentathlon. This was the event that everybody expected the Europeans to dominate, especially seeing as how they had just invented it for this Olympics. It was a beautiful sunny afternoon and I was chomping at the bit to get to it.

Long jump came first. Ferdinand Bie of Norway was the favorite. His best distance was 22 feet 5.7 inches.

"You need to jump twenty-three feet to win," Pop had told me days before. I hadn't been able to practice the long jump on the ship, but I had chalked out that distance on the deck of the S.S. *Finland* and sat staring at it, imagining myself sailing through the air.

And that was what I did that day. I pounded the thirty feet down the track, hit the board, and flew— 23 feet 2.7 inches. I'd won my first event.

Javelin was next and I was only able to take a second behind Hugo Weislander, the Swede who was the world's champion javelin thrower. Second didn't suit me at all. So when the gun cracked for the start of the two hundred meter, I took off like there was no tomorrow and finished first with a time of 22.9 seconds.

In the discus, my throw went three feet farther than Avery Brundage's, and no one else was even close to the two of us. And now all that was left was the fifteen hundred. Despite the fact that I had won three of the first four events, Bie could still win the pentathlon if he took first here and I had a poor showing. The fifteen hundred was his best event and I was not known for long-distance running.

Not only that, they had me in one of the outside lanes. So when we started, I was in poor position and running behind the pack, with Bie and Brundage way up front for the whole first lap. By the middle of the second lap, though, I had passed the rest of the field and was on Bie's heels. Brundage fell back and now it was just me and that speedy Norwegian. I pushed him, running next to him stride for stride. I knew he was famous for his finishing kick and I planned to burn him out before that. On the final lap, I sprinted so far into the lead that it looked like Bie was standing still. I won the fifteen hundred in 4 minutes 44.8 seconds and Bie finished sixth.

The record I set in winning that pentathlon was never broken during the Olympics that followed, and I guess it never will be, seeing as how they stopped running the event sixteen years later. Mr. Sullivan, who I have mentioned before as the head of the AAU, was also the American commissioner for the Olympic Games. That victory of mine tickled him pink.

"Jim's performance," he said, "answers the allegation that most of our runners are of foreign parentage, for Thorpe is a real American if there ever was one."

My next big event was the decathlon, which was not scheduled until the last three days of the games. But I kept busy in the time between. I told Coach Murphy I wanted to take part in the individual events.

"My God, Thorpe," Coach Murphy said, "how many events do you want to enter?"

"All of 'em," I replied. "What's the fun in watching someone else?"

I didn't do as well as I might have done. There was so much going on now and I was getting so much attention that it was a little hard for me to concentrate. I only took fourth in the high jump and seventh in the long jump. But I enjoyed taking part.

One of the other things taking my time was wandering around Stockholm with my new friends.

"What do you think of these Swedish girls?" Abel Kiviat asked me. I had to allow that they were great-looking. But I never really talked to any of them. My mind was on another girl. Each night, when I was back in my bunk, I would write a letter back home to Iva, telling her about the things I'd done and seen and also including more than a few words about how I missed her.

Our team, as a whole, was doing great. Our big men, Ralph Rose, Pat McDonald, and Matthew McGrath, swept the weight events—the two-handed shot, one-handed shot, and hammer throw. Duke Kahanamoku, who swam like a fish, outdistanced everyone in the swimming events. Louis had recovered enough from his seasickness to do well in the five-thousand-meter run.

There, too, no one expected an American to finish near the top. The Finnish runners, the "Flying Finns," were favored for all three places. Johan Kölehmainen was the best and would go on to also win the cross-country and the ten thousand meters. As soon as that five-thousand-meter race started, though, little Louis was on Kölehmainen's heels. He stuck there as long as he could, but just didn't have the strength he needed. Still, even though he only took the silver medal, that race made Louis Tewanima a hero to the fans. They cheered him as much as the winner.

It took so much out of Louis, though, that he wasn't able to do much in the marathon six days later. It was killing weather—so hot and humid that many of the runners couldn't take it. One of them, the Portuguese marathoner Francisco Lázaro, collapsed at mile fourteen. They took him to the hospital, but he never recovered and became the first man to die in the modern Olympics. Louis didn't give up, but the best he could do was sixteenth.

July 13, 1912. Finally it was time for the decathlon. Hugo Weislander of Sweden had won the event three times before and was the big favorite. I felt like I was set, but Pop was worried. A heavy rain was falling and he was sure it would affect me. Pop turned out to be right. I usually ran the hundred in 10 seconds, but that rain slowed me down so much that my time was 11.2 and I took second.

The long-jump track was slippery as all get out. I missed the board and fouled on my first two tries. If that happened again, I'd be out of the competition. I took a deep breath and wiped the rain out of my eyes, then took a high step and ran carefully down the track, hit the board clean, and jumped 22 feet 2.3 inches. I was second again.

"Jim, come with me," Pop said, taking me by the arm before I could head out to the shot put pit.

He took me inside and had me change into a dry tracksuit. "All you have to do is beat Weislander in this one to be on top," Pop said.

That dry suit helped me. My throw of 42 feet 5.9

inches won the shot, a distance two feet farther than Weislander's. At the end of the day after three events, I was on top of the leader board, more than 240 points ahead of Weislander.

The second day was perfect. The sun was shining and there wasn't even a breath of wind. High jump was first. I sailed over the bar at 6 feet 1.6 inches. That was enough to win first place. I was only fourth in the 400 meters, and second in the discus, but I was saving my best for the 110 hurdles. I won that with a time of 15.6 seconds.

On the final day, the event that worried me the most was the pole vault. The best pole-vaulters were wiry little men. I'd seen the wooden poles that we used back then break under the weight of vaulters who were big men like myself. I wasn't sure how it would hold up to my two hundred pounds, so I took it easy. Once I had cleared 10 feet 3 inches, that was enough for me. It was also enough for third place.

I was far ahead of Hugo Weislander now. The only way he could win was if he took the final event and I either failed to finish or came in last. That event was the fifteen hundred meters. I had already won it once in the pentathlon, but some wondered if I could do it again.

They didn't have to wonder for long. I bettered my time by four seconds, winning the fifteen hundred and the decathlon.

The award ceremonies took place on that last day of the games in front of a full stadium. King Gustav himself handed out the gold medals. I came up first to get my award for the pentathlon. I stood there holding my hat over my heart, my back straight and my chin held high. The crowd cheered itself hoarse as King Gustav put a laurel wreath on my head, then

King Gustav V of Sweden presenting Jim with his gold medal in the pentathlon, July 15, 1912

presented me with the medal and also a life-size bronze bust of the king himself. But I wasn't done. I got called back up again for the decathlon. This time, alongside my wreath and gold medal, I was also given a huge silver cup in the shape of a Viking ship. It was all lined with gold and covered with precious jewels and it weighed more than thirty pounds. It was a gift from the czar of Russia.

I was ready to leave the podium, but King Gustav

was not about to let me go yet. He reached out his hand and clasped mine warmly.

His eyes were gleaming and his voice was filled with emotion as he spoke those words that I will never forget.

"Sir," he said, "you are the greatest athlete in the world."

That was the proudest moment of my life. The king kept looking in my eyes, shaking my hand. I guessed I ought to say something. So I did.

"Thanks, King," I said.

36

ALL KINDS OF OPPORTUNITIES

I didn't head for home right away. I'd been asked to stay with the team for three special meets for the Olympians. So I went on to Reims and Paris with Abel and the others to run a few races. I didn't have a cent on me, so when the other boys went out to have a beer, I'd just sit with them and drink water. But I didn't mind that at all. I was seeing things I'd never imagined I'd see.

In fact, the only race I lost was because of that. In Paris I was halfway through the hurdles when a plane flew low over the stadium. I'd never seen an airplane before and I just had to look up at it, which caused me to stub my toe on a hurdle and fall flat. I laid there and watched that plane pass over while the rest of the runners kept going. That plane was really something!

When we got back home we were treated like we were kings ourselves. There was a big parade in New York City for the whole Olympic team. It was said that there were a million people watching us go by in a car caravan down Fifth Avenue. Then in Philadelphia there was another parade just for the Pennsylvania athletes, and a banquet afterward, where I got to sit down with the most famous baseball player in the world, Ty Cobb.

Finally, though, we all got back to Carlisle. It was Friday, August 16 when Pop and Louis and I stepped off the midday train at the station to be greeted by a big crowd waving banners that said such things as HAIL TO CHIEF THORPE and THE GREATEST COACH IN THE WORLD. We were loaded into a horse-drawn carriage, driven by none other than my old friend Mr. Pope. He tipped his hat and winked at me, then clucked to his horses, and we were off. Marching behind us were not just the platoons of our Carlisle cadets in their uniforms, but every organization in the whole Cumberland Valley. The Empire Hook and Ladder, the Mount Holly fire department, the Steelton band—they were all there to follow us through town. The streets was hung with bunting and more signs welcoming us, and people were out waving and cheering. We ended up at Dickinson College's Biddle Field, where about five thousand people watched from the stands as Superintendent Friedman stood up to read a letter written to me by the President of the United States himself.

My Dear Sir:

I have much pleasure in congratulating you on account of your noteworthy victory at the Olympic Games in Stockholm. Your performance is one of which you may well be proud. You have set a high standard of physical development which is only attained by right living and right thinking, and your victory will serve as an

incentive to all to improve those qualities which
characterize the best type of American citizen.
It is my earnest wish that the future will bring
you success in your chosen field of endeavor.

Sincerely Yours,
William Howard Taft

That event in Carlisle was my favorite of my return, even though it seemed as if the whole world was celebrating my victory. Every newspaper in the country carried stories about my winning those two gold medals. Down in North Carolina, the *Charlotte Observer* had even run a story on July 18, 1912, bragging of how "Big Chief Thorpe" of the Carolina league had been "a sensation at the bag" during my two seasons of summer ball when Charley Clancy was my manager.

You might have thought that I would hear something from the Bureau of Indian Affairs, too. However, the only word that came from my Indian agency in Oklahoma was a three-word message. Superintendent Friedman, who somehow had never realized that my parents had passed away years ago, had contacted the agency to try to invite my parents to be there to celebrate my homecoming. The telegram he got back read: "Thorpe's Parents Dead."

All my friends and teammates were gathered around that day and it was glorious. The only thing that made me a little sad was that Iva couldn't be there. After she had graduated in the spring, her aunt and her other relatives had come and taken her out to California. Even though she had gotten her education in an Indian school, they didn't think much of her association with an Indian athlete. They had taken away the engagement ring I gave her and advised her to forget about any ideas of ever marrying me.

The final thing that day was when they asked each of us, Pop, Louis, and me, to stand up and say a few words. Pop went first, speaking at some length. When it was my turn, I kept it short. I looked out at the crowd, grinned, and then declared, "All I can say is that you showed me a good time."

Louis, though, went me one better. I'd heard it said—and it was even reported in the *Red Man*—that Louis's entire speech was "Me, too." But his address to the waiting crowd was longer than that. He stood up, looked around at everyone, and then said in a soft voice: "I thank you."

Now that his five years were done at Carlisle, Louis was finally free to go home. He spent a few days on campus, saying good-bye to friends and handing out a few souvenirs he'd picked up in his travels. He also gave away most of the track medals and ribbons he'd won during his years of running races. Some of the girls at Carlisle turned those medals into buckles that they proudly wore on their shoes. About all that Louis took home with him was his certificate from the tailor shop and his Olympic silver medal. He went back to Hopi to live out his life. As far as I know he is still there, up on Second Mesa, wearing his red headband and his silver and turquoise earrings, planting his corn, and following the Hopi way.

As for me, I had all kinds of opportunities now. There was baseball teams that wanted to sign me right away to a professional contract. A famous promoter, Mr. Cash-and-Carry Pyle, offered me a contract of ten thousand dollars to go on tour with him around the country.

"Take it," Gus Welch said. "That's more money than I'll ever see."

I was tempted. I was also broke. Against his better judgment, my Indian agent had finally sent me all that was left in my account—$295 that he told me I could "use without restriction."

Pop Warner, though, had other plans for me.

"Jim," he said, "speaking as your coach, your adviser, and your friend, I think you should stay an amateur for one more season. Come back to the gridiron for your final year. We have fourteen games scheduled, and—with you on our roster—a chance to be the number one team in America. Another season of football will boost your market value when it comes time to negotiate with the baseball clubs. You could also finish your certificate."

It was always hard to argue with Pop. In my heart I knew he was right, even if there was nothing in my pocketbook. And since I was staying an amateur, I could also take part in the big end-of-summer AAU track meet in New York City on September 2.

I almost didn't make it, though. At one of the parties that took place after I got back, I had eaten something that didn't agree with me. I came down with food poisoning and ended up in the hospital. But despite the fact that I was still feeling weak and woozy, I checked myself out the day before the meet and took the train to New York. My head was spinning the whole way and I just about fell down when I got off on the platform in New York. That wasn't the end of it, though. When I got there to Celtic Park, it was my favorite kind of day—cold and rainy. But after all I'd gone through to get there, I wasn't about to quit. I competed in ten events in one day, won most of them, set a record in the hurdles, and got the trophy as the All-Around Athlete.

Mr. Sullivan wanted me to take part in a whole string of other meets all across the country. I thanked him for his offer, but I had other plans. "I have trained hard for this meet and now need a rest, which I will take immediately," I told the reporters.

That rest lasted about two weeks, until our home opener on September 21.

37

THE 1912 SEASON

"Well, there's one thing I like about this new field," I said to Gus Welch on our first day of practice. "Now that it's only a hundred yards, it won't tire us out so much running for touchdowns."

Just like the year before, the 1912 season brought more rule changes to the game of football. The length of the football field was shortened to what it is today and an extra ten yards was added behind each goal as a passing zone. We also now had four downs, rather than three, to gain ten yards and a first down. Field goals were still three points, but a touchdown was now worth six, with the kick making it a total of seven. That dumb rule limiting the forward pass to twenty yards had been dumped back into the trash can where it belonged. Tripping was no longer allowed and there were stiffer penalties for unnecessary roughness. Every one of those changes was a good one and sure to help the wide-open style of play we favored at Carlisle.

One place where there weren't any changes was in our starting backfield. All four of us, Gus, Alex, Possum, and me were back again. So was our center, Joe Bergie, and our two guards, Bill Garlow and Big Bear Elmer Busch. Of course we also still had our coach. Pop Warner was there on the field with us, planning new strategies that would include, in the year of 1912, a double-wing formation that no one had ever seen before but would become a standard part of football in the years to come.

There were changes to the rest of the team, though. Billy Newashe was back in Oklahoma and gone from tackle. I wouldn't play ball with him again until years later in the pros—where a lot of us Carlisle Indians came back together to have some more fun. Bill Lone Star Dietz was still at Carlisle, but as an assistant coach. We'd also lost both our ends. Sam Burd had finished his studies, while Henry Roberts had gone back into a government job, this time at the Shoshoni Agency way out in Wind River, Wyoming.

Those who filled in at those positions were more than up to the task. Even though they were both undersized, Roy Large, a Shoshone, and Cotton Vetternack did a fine job as our two starting ends, with Joel Williams getting about as much playing time there, too. For our tackles, we had two of our biggest boys at 195 pounds each. Both of them liked carrying the ball and would end up in that role in the years to come. But Pete Calac, who was a Mission Indian from California and Joe Guyon, another Chippewa, willingly threw their bodies into the line that year. We also had some fine backups as ballcarriers, especially Bruce Goesback and Hugh Wheelock.

In fact, in our first two warm-up games, it was those backups who did the playing. Pop had decided to save me and most of the starters for the most challenging games. I hate to think what the scores would have been if I had played. In our home opener Albright was whipped by a score of 40–7, and a few days later poor little Lebanon Valley went down 45–0. I probably would have had at least ten more touchdowns that season.

I did finally get into the Dickinson game the next weekend. As always, they played us tough, and the first quarter went scoreless. Then, the first time I touched the pigskin in the second quarter, I went twenty-five yards up the middle for a touchdown. They held our boys on the next series of downs and we were pushed back deep into our own side of the field. Pop signaled me in to punt. Joe Bergie was usually a great snapper, but not this time. The ball sailed over my head all the way back into the end zone. I ran back to get it and found myself in my own end zone surrounded by most of the Dickinson eleven. Pop was signaling for me to take a knee and accept a safety, but I had another idea. I sidestepped one man, let two others crash into each other, jumped over a third, knocked over a fourth, and I was on my way. A hundred and nine yards later, I was in the opposite end zone touching the ball to the grass—34–0 was the final score.

We only had three days' rest before the Villanova game, a 65 to 0 Carlisle win where I played less than twenty minutes—time enough for me to score three touchdowns. Aside from kicking the extra

points, I spent the rest of the game on the sidelines. I wasn't even able to watch the action because I was surrounded by hundreds of folks, from little kids to old men and women, who came crowding up to shake my hand or get my autograph. I finally had to move to the clubhouse so that all my fans wouldn't spill onto the field of play.

Washington and Jefferson, the fifth team on our schedule in only three weeks, was a different story and it's not one that I'm proud of. Even though they were a small school, they were on their way toward building themselves into a powerhouse. Ten thousand people came to their little campus to see our contest. They were good, but good as they were, we really beat ourselves—none of us Carlisle Indians played up to our ability. I got praised for the four interceptions I made that kept them from scoring and my punts were averaging sixty yards or more. But I missed on all three of my field goal attempts and it ended up a scoreless tie—o–o. I felt like I'd let myself and the whole team down.

October 12 was at Syracuse. It meant a lot to all of us, since they had spoiled our run toward a perfect season the year before. However, our old friends the mud and the rain were waiting for us when we got there. Every time I tried running around the end, my feet slipped and I wasn't able to gain ground before being tackled.

"Where's your sense, Jim?" Pop said to me. "Don't you see that speed is going to get you nowhere on

this slippery ground? For heaven's sake, use your weight."

I took Pop's advice and stopped trying those end runs. I just ran straight bucks or off tackle. I tallied three touchdowns in our 33–0 shutout.

Part of the reason our line did so well that day was the way Big Bear played at guard. Elmer Busch was a big amiable guy and it was sometimes hard to get him inspired. About the only time Elmer got tough was when he was angry that someone on the other side was playing dirty against him. So, near the start of every game Big Bear would end up getting pushed from behind or hit in the back of his head.

"Who did that?" Elmer would roar.

"Looks like it was that boy right there," Gus would answer, pointing out the player opposite Elmer on the other team. "You go get him next play."

"By gosh, I will do just that!" Big Bear would snarl with fire in his eyes.

All season no man on our team ever got fouled as much as Elmer. He was pushed and kicked, punched and tripped—and even bitten on the leg once in a pileup. No matter how much he complained to the officials about it, the players on the other side would always deny it. The fact that the officials wouldn't listen to him made Big Bear even angrier, often to the point where he was just about unstoppable. He would flatten out whoever he thought had fouled him on the next play and then growl, "Let that be a lesson to you."

"Well, Elmer," Gus said after our last game together, "how did you enjoy your football? Did you get anything out of the game?"

Big Bear shook his head. "I tell you, Gus, I used to enjoy the game. But I never saw so many dirty white men!"

Gus started to laugh and so did all of the rest of us who had been in on the joke all along. "Elmer," Gus said, "I've got a confession. All those times you got kicked and punched and hit, the one doing it was me. It was the only way I could get you to play your hardest."

Big Bear stood there silent for a while. Finally he shook his head. "Gus," he said, "you are a smart quarterback. But I guess I ought to go and apologize now to those officials."

The University of Pittsburgh was October 19. Pop showed me a clipping from one of the Pittsburgh papers. "Thorpe will never run through us," it read. "We've got him figured." Bragging always inspired me the same way rough play fired up Big Bear. I scored thirty-four points as we flattened Pitt in a 45–8 rout.

The Georgetown game on October 26 was a more interesting trip for us because we were a bunch of Indians going into Washington, DC. Washington means something different to Indians than it does to other Americans. It is the place where the decisions have been made for years that have meant life and death to our tribes. Anything that happened in

Washington was political, even a football game. None other than Senator Boies Penrose of Pennsylvania came to visit us in our dressing room before the game. The Carlisle School Appropriation Bill was before Congress that week. He figured that a Carlisle victory would help push it through.

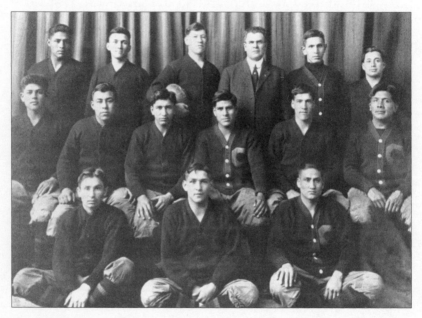

The 1912 Carlisle Football Team. Top row (left to right): Charles Williams, Gus Welch, Jim Thorpe, Pop Warner, Robert Hill, William Garlow. Middle row: Pete Calac, Joe Bergie, Joel Wheelock, Stansil "Possum" Powell, Joe Guyon, Elmer Busch. Bottom row: George Vetterneck, Roy Large, Alex Arcasa.

"Thorpe," the senator said to me, "you go out there and play a great game, we might make you a citizen of this great country." Then he turned to Gus and grabbed his hand. "Welch, if you go out there and call a smart game, *you* could become a citizen."

Neither one of us said a thing. We both appreciated the irony of Indians who weren't even allowed to vote and were treated like children by the Bureau of Indian Affairs being asked to help out a senator. In fact, it would be twelve years before Congress passed the Indian Citizenship Bill that finally allowed the original Americans to call themselves citizens of their own homeland, and Senator Penrose had nothing to do with it.

Citizens or not, we played a strong game that day against a tough team and won 34–20. Gus got something even more out of that game than a team victory. Our Oklahoma Congressman, Charles Carter, came to the game with his daughter Julia. Congressman Carter had been a member of the Chickasaw Tribal Council before being elected to Congress and he invited our whole team to his home after the game. The friendship that Julia struck up with Gus would end up with their being married in 1923.

The game that followed Georgetown was more fun than anything else. In the middle of the week we went to Toronto to play against an all-star Canadian rugby team. It was the hundredth anniversary of the War of 1812 and also the week of the Canadian Thanksgiving, and the attendance was big enough to guarantee Pop Warner a three-thousand-dollar share of the gate. The first half of the game was played with U.S. football rules. For the second half, we decided to play according to Canadian rules. When it was all done, we'd won 49–1.

November 2 was Lehigh. Their quarterback, Pazetti, was an All-American, and they planned on beating us with their passing game. On the first set of downs they drove down the field while we hung back, wanting to see how they were running their plays, until they got about to our ten-yard line. Then Pazetti dropped back and threw into the end zone—where I was waiting. I intercepted the ball ten yards behind the goal and wove my way through the Lehigh team. I thought I was in the clear when I heard feet pounding behind me. I looked back to see Pazetti trying to catch me. I smiled back at him, laughed, and started to run in earnest, leaving him far behind as I took the ball in for a 110-yard score.

They scored twice themselves and didn't play badly at all. As a matter of fact, as I often did in games, I patted quite a few of them on the back and said "Good play" after picking them up from where I'd tackled them. But in the long run, we had their number. In fact, we started telling them our own numbers. "How about number twelve through left tackle?" I'd yell. And that was where I'd run. "Right end, huh?" I'd shout. Bam! Straight over the right end. At first they thought we were trying to trick them, but even after they caught on that we were serious, they still couldn't stop us. That game was really fun, with a final score of 34–14.

We knew, though, that we had to be serious in the battle that lay ahead of us on the banks of the Hudson River. The Indians were going up against the Army.

For Pop Warner, football always was war. In his famous football guidebook he wrote:

Each scrimmage represents a battle in which the opposing forces are lined up opposite each other, one side defending itself against the attack of the other. The lines represent the infantry, and the backs can be likened to cavalry, quick moving and able to charge the enemy at any spot, or rush to the support of the position attacked.

He wanted his players to be deadly serious, and he sometimes lost patience with the way we would have fun on the field. So Pop did everything he could to get us up for the West Point game. He paced back and forth in the locker room while we stood up on the benches.

"Boys," he said, "it was the fathers and grandfathers of these men who fought the Indians. But this time the contest between red men and white can be waged on equal terms."

He really did get us keyed up and I suppose we needed it that day. Army was the heavy favorite, having slammed its way through some of the best teams in the East. Those Army boys were huge, too. They just towered over us and way outweighed us. Our team averaged out at 170 pounds, and at 71.2 inches I was the tallest player on our squad. Leland Devore, their 250-pound captain, was an All-American tackle, and they had a halfback named

Dwight Eisenhower who was dynamite on both offense and defense.

The first thing we did was to come out in a formation no one had ever seen before. Pop Warner called it the "single wing," and it had me at left half, moved up close to the line. That way I could run, block, or throw. It confused the heck out of the Army players. On our first play Alex made fifteen yards. Then I went around end for eighteen. Then Possum plowed through the center for eight. Then I went off tackle for twenty.

On the Army side, Eisenhower and the other backs brought the ball all the way downfield and took it in for a score, but missed the extra point. We answered with a touchdown of our own and I kicked the extra point, giving us a 7–6 edge when the first half ended.

In the second half, we really took control. I was running the ball when I saw Eisenhower and another West Point player zeroing in on me. I stopped short and they hit each other with a crash like two freight trains colliding. They were both so woozy that their coach took them out of the game and neither one came back in again.

I had one long touchdown run called back when Cotton was penalized for holding, and my only scoring was in my extra points. But I played just as well at defense that day. We stopped the Army players cold for the rest of that game and ended up the winners by a score of 27–6. That was the second of the two best games I ever played in college.

Even though they lost, those Army men were great sports and gave us credit for what we did. Leland Devore overdid it a bit in what he said about me to the reporters, but I sure smiled when I read it.

That Indian is the greatest player I have ever stacked up against in my five years experience. He is super-human, that is all. There is nothing he can't do. He kicks superbly, worms his way through a field like a combination of greyhound, jackrabbit and eel. He is as cunning and strategic as a fox. He follows interference like the hangers-on follow an army.

Dwight Eisenhower, who would go on to be the Supreme Allied Commander in World War II, was darn kind, too. He said: "Thorpe was able to do everything that anyone else could, but he could do it better."

Despite the fact that we'd won, that Army game had been a war for us and we'd taken casualties. We went into Philadelphia for the University of Pennsylvania game worn out and letting down. Penn had already lost three games and we were favored, but they were the giant killers that day. We just plain beat ourselves with fumbles. Even though we had 400 yards to their 177, we lost our first game of the season 34–26.

Our second-to-last game was supposed to be little more than a scrimmage, but Springfield YMCA College in Massachusetts was better than we'd expected. We had to work hard to come up the winners 30–24.

For me, though, the most important thing that happened that day was not on the playing field. I didn't even know about it at the time, but one of the men watching our game was Charley Clancy, who had been my summer ball manager in Fayetteville, North Carolina. Charley was now managing the Winston-Salem team in the new Eastern Carolina League, but he was spending the off season with friends in Southbridge, Massachusetts.

"I know that guy," Charley said to a reporter friend of his as I passed them on the sidelines. "He played baseball for me a couple of years ago."

38

EVERYTHING COMES TO AN END

Everything comes to an end someday. That's what our Sac and Fox elders say, and suddenly I was facing the end of my career as a football player for the Carlisle Indians. The final game of our season was November 30 against our old rivals, Brown University. When we took the field that day, our long red capes swirling around us as we ran across the frozen turf, I knew we had a tough row to hoe. Gus Welch was too hurt to play and an icy wind was whipping snow around us. Once again, we were the underdogs. We had lost to Penn. This Brown team had whomped them 30–7. The general opinion in the press was that we didn't stand a chance.

Pop moved Joe Bergie, our center, to fullback. Joe Garlow slid over to center. Alex Arcasa played quarterback. Hugh Wheelock and Bruce Goesback alternated on one side of the backfield. As always, I was at the other halfback position. My kicking game suffered from the snow and that swirling wind. I missed two field goals and my punts were short, but we held Brown scoreless through the first half even though we felt like icicles when we trudged into the locker room.

Pop Warner looked at our discouraged faces. "Boys,"

he said, "this is Jim Thorpe's last game. You owe him a victory for the many games he won for you."

I guess that short speech worked. We played that second half like a house on fire. I began making long gains on the ground, including a 110-yard touchdown when we faked a punt behind our own goal line. I even connected on three passes, including a touchdown to Joe Guyon. On my last play of the game, I took a direct snap from Joe Garlow and galloped eighteen yards for a touchdown through the hole that Possum and Joe Guyon opened. It was my third touchdown of the day, my twenty-fifth of the season. All in all, I scored 198 points that year for Carlisle.

The last game was a great team effort for us all, even though the boxed headlines in more than one newspaper read "The Real Score: Thorpe . . . 32, Brown . . . 0." It was just about a perfect way to end my college career.

Now that the season was over, I was getting all kinds of offers to sign one sort of pro contract or another, most of them for more money than I'd ever dreamed of. Five different Major League Baseball teams all wanted me to play for them, thinking that my name would draw people to the sport, which was suffering from poor attendance.

Pop urged me to stay on through the spring for another track season and to get my certificate. The AAU was after me to take part in a whole series of meets as an amateur. What I really wanted to do, though, was go back home for a while and think things over. I had lots of options now and I felt good about them. I still had less than three hundred dollars to my name, but I figured the future was bright. I had no idea that the storm I'd played through on the field in Providence was mild compared to the one that was about to break and bring an end to my amateur career forever.

The only thing that kept me from being completely happy was that my girl Iva was still in California. But at least her relatives were allowing her to write back to me now.

The week after the Brown game I was chosen again by Walter Camp as a first-team All-American halfback, and I was granted a leave by Carlisle to spend my holidays in Oklahoma. I wanted to take my Olympic gold medals and my other prizes I'd won with me, but Pop didn't think it was a good idea.

"Let me just hold on to them for you, Jim," he said. "They'll be safer with me."

I wish now I had known how wrong he was about that.

Back home, though, I was given a hero's welcome. All the papers in Oklahoma had been following the incredible year I'd enjoyed. Just about everywhere I went people from all different tribes came up and shook my hand and told me I'd done myself proud. Old people blessed me with tobacco and eagle feathers and prayed in Indian, saying that what I had accomplished was not just for myself, but for every Indian, for our ancestors and those yet to come. There were times when I had tears in my eyes as people went on about what an example I was for our children, how I gave hope to all.

Of course, the best times were those I spent with Mary and my brother Frank and our whole extended family. It was just wall-to-wall Thorpes some days and I was happy as a hog in a wallow.

On January 18, I returned to Carlisle, just in time for the annual reception and dance of the Mercer Society, one of our student social clubs. There was a dance contest, and Clemence La Traille, who had danced with me a time or two before, agreed to be my partner. We got first place in the two-step.

Gus Welch teased me as they gave me the prize, which was a big chocolate cake. "Well, Jim," he said, "it appears you are going to have your cake and eat it, too." We all laughed, but that was the last laughing I would do for a while.

DISGRACE

I no longer remember who handed me the paper as I entered the reading room in the football quarters. But I do remember the sick feeling in my stomach as I read it.

THORPE WITH PROFESSIONAL
BASEBALL TEAM SAYS CLANCY

That was the headline in the *Worcester Telegram* on January 22, 1913. The piece that followed explained what that meant. Because I had been paid to play baseball, I had given up my amateur status before returning to Carlisle for my last two years of football. Being a professional athlete disqualified me from taking part in the Olympic Games.

The article was unsigned, but I learned later that the reporter was a man named Roy Johnson. He was the same person who had heard Charley Clancy identify me at the Springfield game as one of his former players. He had gone south to follow up on the story and had seen that team photo in Charley's office. It was Roy Johnson's chance at breaking a big story and he took it. The spark of that story started a fire that spread to every paper in the country.

247

What did earning a few bucks playing summer ball have to do with track and field? How was it any different from earning summer money hoeing potatoes? It was hard for me to understand. But what bothered me most about that story was the stuff that Mr. Clancy, my old team manager, was quoted as having said.

It was true that I'd played in North Carolina, but not at Winston-Salem, like the article reported. The worst things it had wrong were about me and my character. It talked about my having white ancestry as if it meant I was not a real Indian. It reported Mr. Clancy as having said that I was a coward and a drunk and that I used to walk down Main Street with a gallon jug in my hand, stopping every now and then to take a swig and let out a war whoop. It even described how I supposedly jumped through the plate glass window of a saloon and then did the same thing again at a grocery store where the glass scalped me right on top of my head.

None of that ever happened. Not ever. Charley Clancy himself tried to set the record straight that he had never said those bad things about me. He had told Roy Johnson that I was a fine player and a reliable person. But I guess Mr. Johnson was not going to let the truth get in the way of a good story. The whole tone was nasty, and papers all over the country picked it up and repeated those mean untruths. I suppose there are some people who believe them to this day.

When Pop called me in to meet with him, what I

wanted to talk about was the way that unsigned article was lying about me. Would it destroy my reputation? What about all the Indian kids who looked up to me? What would they think?

But Pop silenced me. "We've got a bigger problem, Jim," he said. "If you were paid to play baseball, then your amateur standing is in question."

"What do you mean 'if,' Pop?" I said. I was flabbergasted. "You knew all about me and lots of other Carlisle athletes playing summer ball. Everybody did. Even Mr. Sullivan of the AAU talked about my being a great baseball player."

Pop shook his head. "Jim," he said, "we have to deny it."

I didn't understand why, but that was what Pop did—backed by Mr. Sullivan of the AAU.

An interview with Pop was printed in the *New York Times* on January 25.

"All I know about the charges about Mr. Thorpe have been gleaned from the newspaper reports to the effect that a Mr. Clancy, manager of a Southern ball team, has been quoted as saying that Thorpe played professional baseball with a Winston-Salem team under his management," Pop said. Then he went on to quote from a signed letter written to him by Charley Clancy denying I had ever played in any position in the Carolina league or been paid any money for playing. Pop ended his interview by stating, "I am further assured by Thorpe that there is nothing in the story."

It made me feel even sicker to my stomach. They were all telling lies about lies. I just wanted to tell the truth, but they wouldn't let me. My Sac and Fox elders had always told me to be truthful. Once you start lying, you just keep on lying. It's like crawling out on a limb and starting to cut it off behind you. Sooner or later that branch is going to break and you are going to fall.

Sure enough, despite what Pop and the others said, the story refused to go away. There were plenty of records about my being in North Carolina, everything from payrolls to newspaper articles, as well as the word of people I played with down there. Within a few days the story about my disgrace was being featured in papers all over the country.

Pop called me to his office again to discuss strategy.

"I don't understand, Pop," I said. "What's two months of baseball got to do with all the running and jumping and field work I did in Stockholm? I never got paid for any of that, did I? And what about all the other college boys who play summer ball for pay? College students from all over the country do it and then go back to being amateurs. Nobody is going after *them*."

"They're trying to force you into becoming a professional, Jim," Pop replied. "I think this whole thing is the doing of baseball scouts trying to force you out of the amateur ranks. This is all planned to get them free advertising and you to sign a contract."

I shook my head. It was what I'd always wanted—a contract to play professional ball. But I didn't want it this way, not with my name dragged in the mud.

"What can I do?" I asked.

"Ride it out, Jim. There are too many people out there who love you for this to ruin your career. You'll still come out a winner."

Pop may have been right, but the worst was still to come. If it was proved that Pop knew about my playing summer ball for pay, then *his* career would be finished, too. People would also take a close look at the whole Carlisle football system, including all the money brought in by those gate receipts and the payments Pop made to his players over the years. That was the last thing Pop Warner wanted to have come out in the open. Carlisle would have to fire him and he'd never coach again.

Superintendent Friedman was also worried. He was the one who had given me leave, according to the Carlisle records, to play summer ball. He was already being questioned about his running of Carlisle. In fact, in another year, a scandal would break about his mismanagement that would end up in congressional hearings and lead him to resign from his post. This whole matter had to end, the sooner the better. Then there was also the AAU. If it turned out that they also knew about my summer ball career, such important people as Mr. Sullivan could lose their jobs, too.

On January 26, I was called in to meet with Pop and

Superintendent Friedman. They handed me a letter. I read it over and then looked up at Pop.

"It's the only way, Jim," he said. "If you confess, then this whole thing can be put behind us. You still have a bright future ahead of you."

"Copy it over in your own hand," Superintendent Friedman said, handing me a pen and another piece of paper.

"Trust me, Jim," Pop said.

So I did. Why? Maybe because Pop was my coach and he said I should do it. After years of taking a coach's advice, most successful athletes will tell you that it's hard not to go along with something that they tell you is for your own good and for the good of the team.

And what choice did I have? It didn't matter that I was the best-known athlete in the world and a sports hero. I was still just one little Indian boy from Oklahoma. If I had tried to speak up against Pop Warner and Carlisle and the AAU, I wouldn't have stood a chance. I am pretty sure that there would have been no career for me in baseball or any other sport after that.

It galled me, but I did what I was told. I copied the letter over and signed it, and it was taken to the AAU and published in the papers. Some of it was true, like my admitting I had played for pay at Rocky Mount and Fayetteville and hadn't known there was anything wrong about doing it. But some of it, like the parts where I said that I never told anyone about it and kept it all secret from Pop Warner, was just plain false. I'd never lied before, and for years after, whenever anyone asked me about that confession and what really happened, I always answered by saying, "That is all behind me now."

40

THINGS COME AROUND

My letter was not the only one written that day. Superintendent Friedman sent one to the AAU, too.

"I have just learned," the superintendent wrote, "that Thorpe acknowledges having played with a Southern professional baseball team. It is with profound regret that this information is conveyed to you, and I hasten to assure your committee that the faculty of the school and the athletic director, Mr. Glenn Warner, were without any knowledge of this fact until today."

It was all my fault, and the only thing that could excuse me was that I was just a dumb Indian who didn't understand the rules. That was the whole of Pop Warner and Superintendent Friedman's defense. Pop laid it out in an interview he gave the papers after that confession that they wrote for me became public.

"In a way," Pop told the reporters, "the boys at the Indian school were children mentally and did not understand the fine distinctions between amateurism and professionalism."

Some people might think I was too innocent and trusting when I agreed to write that letter, but I did it with my eyes wide open. Before I went in to that meeting with Pop and the superintendent, I had one of my own with Gus Welch and Sam Burd—who was still in the area, taking courses at Conway Hall, even though he'd graduated from Carlisle—and some of my other friends.

"Don't sign anything," Gus said.

Sam agreed. "Any time an Indian signs a paper a white man gives him, he ends up losing. Think of all our treaties."

I understood what they were saying, but I also had my own way of thinking about it. You know how stubborn I am. As far as the superintendent went, I didn't much care for him—nor did anyone by then, neither students nor faculty. But I was afraid this whole thing could hurt Carlisle and Pop. I truly didn't want that to happen. And, like I said, I felt like I didn't have any other choice.

So Pop took my confession and the superintendent's letter and headed to New York City to meet with the AAU Olympic selection committee—which really meant that he and his good friend Mr. Sullivan talked over what should be done to clear themselves and wash their hands of the whole deal. The best way for the AAU to protect itself was for them to condemn me as proof of their own innocence. If they were too lenient, it might look suspicious. And whatever was done had to be done fast, like swatting a mosquito before it bites you. So there wasn't any hearing or investigation or trial, just Mr. Sullivan's iron hand coming down hard.

"Mr. Thorpe," Sullivan said, "is deserving of the severest condemnation for concealing the fact that he professionalized himself." My name, Sullivan announced, was to be removed from the record books and my trophies to be sent back to the Swedish Olympic Committee to be given to the second-place finishers. It was just that easy.

The news spread fast. On January 28, the front-page headline in the *New York Times* read:

Olympic prizes lost: Thorpe no amateur

It about broke my heart to read that headline. But what happened over the next few days surprised me. One or two papers criticized me, but not many. In fact, the opinion of most was that the AAU was wrong in their decision. Some of the articles in the newspapers treated the whole matter with disdain. They said I was being done an injustice. Just like me, they wondered what connection there was between baseball and track. The *Philadelphia Inquirer* ran a story saying that "all aspiring athletes would do well to ponder this action of the Amateur Athletic Union and not play croquet, ping-pong, tiddly-winks, or button-button-who's-got-the-button for compensation. It puts them in the ranks of professionals and absolutely disqualifies them from being able to run, jump, hurdle, throw the discus, pole vault, or wrestle." It also asked what the AAU planned to do about "college athletes that are given their tuition free and receive special favors on the side in order that their services on the football field and in track events may be utilized."

The piece I liked best, which I pasted into my scrapbook on a page all its own, was in the *Buffalo Enquirer*. It said that I was the greatest athlete in the world. They might "take away Thorpe's tin medals and pieces of pottery, but the honest world would always consider him the athlete par excellence of the past fifty years."

Damon Runyon, who was the most famous sportswriter of the time, said that even if the AAU took my records out of the books it would never remove them from the memory of the people.

In the end, just about everyone sympathized with me. I think even Pop Warner was surprised by the groundswell of public opinion in my favor. It was as true in Europe as it was in the United States. Even the Swedish Olympic Committee went so far as to state that I was entitled to retain the prizes I won. Let Thorpe keep his medals. That was what just about everyone was saying now all around the world.

But Mr. Sullivan was not about to back down. Finally, under pressure from the AAU and the U.S. Olympic Committee, the International Olympic Committee agreed in May of 1913 to ratify the AAU's decision to strip me of my Olympic honors. Pop Warner handed over my trophies to the AAU, where they were crated up and shipped off to the IOC headquarters in Switzerland. I never saw my medals and trophies again.

It was clear I was going to have to leave Carlisle. My days as a college athlete had been ended by the scandal. I packed up my bag, shook hands with my friends and teachers, and went down to Indian Field for one last time. I stood there all alone, watching the snow swirl over the gridiron that had been watered over the years with so much Indian sweat and blood and tears. Then I turned and walked away without looking back until I had passed through the school gate. The final entry about me in my Carlisle record was a short one: "2-1-13 discharged to play ball."

Tough as the last few weeks had been for me, I was no longer feeling sick at heart. The outpouring of support had given me back my self-esteem. And it seemed that, just as Pop had promised, I had a bright future ahead of me after all. Despite having my Olympic honors taken from me, I was getting all kinds of offers. The biggest one was from Harry Edwards, a Philadelphia promoter, who guaranteed me fifty thousand dollars if I would sign a contract to become a professional prizefighter. The vaudeville and lecture circuits wanted me to travel the country, giving talks and performing feats of strength on stage for a thousand dollars a week. Theatrical agents and motion picture moguls were writing me, sending me telegrams, inviting me to meet with them.

Those were all great offers, but what I really wanted to do was play ball. I probably could have been a fair boxer and I had come to be at ease when it came to talking to a crowd. But the idea of hitting other men with my fists for a living or standing up on the stage didn't sound like fun.

Six major-league ball clubs all offered me a contract. With all those different teams bidding for me, I needed some help.

"I'll be your agent, Jim," Pop Warner said.

Well, who else would I have gone to? Plus I knew that as my agent, he would try to get the best possible contract so that both of us would benefit. There was no doubt that Pop Warner knew the world of money better than I did.

We talked over all of the offers. Finally, Pop and I settled on the New York Giants. They was the best team in the world that year and they offered me the biggest contract ever paid to a rookie: six thousand dollars a year for three years. That would be like a million-dollar contract today. Sure, it was less than I might have earned in vaudeville, but it was more money than most men ever earned in a lifetime. My teachers at Carlisle only got paid about six hundred dollars a year, and Pop Warner himself only got four thousand dollars a year.

I thought it was a great deal. Best of all, I would be back on a ball field and not up on a stage.

Of course Pop made out just fine from being my agent. He got a whopping big commission of twenty-five hundred dollars.

That day put a smile back on my face and my sense

of humor returned with it. After I signed, reporters crowded around me.

"What's your Indian name?" one of them asked.

"Drags His Foot," I said.

Pop hastened to take the man to the side before he wrote that down to explain that I was joking. "Jim does not know his real Indian name," Pop explained. Or at least Pop Warner didn't.

"What was your greatest experience in all your years of sports?" another asked.

"Well," I said, holding my hands out, "when I was a boy back in Oklahoma, I caught a fish that was this big!"

"No," the reporter said. "I mean your most memorable experience in sports."

"Oh," I said, holding my hands a little farther apart, "in that case it was last summer when I caught a fish that was *this* big."

They also asked that question I'd been expecting.

"What do you have to say about their taking away your Olympic medals, Jim?"

"I've said all I have to say about it," I replied. "That is in the past."

When we got back to Carlisle, a crowd was waiting for us. They had signs that said things like STILL THE WORLD'S GREATEST ATHLETE, and they were waving Carlisle banners.

Mr. Blumenthal, the haberdasher who had made my suits, and Frank Farabelli, who ran the fruit stand, and Colonel Miller from the Chocolate Shop, and nearly all the other Carlisle merchants were there. Mr. Blumenthal had a big grin on his face and was holding a jar full of money.

"Jim," he said, "we been taking up a collection in the town. We are going to purchase a trophy in your honor to take the place of those ones they made you give back."

I felt so honored that I almost cried. Just about everybody in town had been contributing, putting in their pennies and nickels and dimes. But when I shook their hands, I also shook my head.

"Those trophies are gone," I said. "I don't want another one. Please give the money you've collected to charity."

That was a great day. And what made it even better was the letter that I had in my pocket from California. Not only did Iva write how proud she was of me, she also said that she would soon be coming back east so that we could plan our future together.

Our marriage took place on October 14, 1913, at Carlisle. Gus Welch was my best man, and because Iva's parents were deceased, Superintendent Friedman gave the bride away.

"Iva," I told her after we said our vows, "the king of Sweden called me Sir. I guess that means I'm a Lord and if I'm a Lord, then you are my Lady."

Then we went on a royal honeymoon. It took us around the world, where I played exhibition baseball games in England, France, Italy, Egypt, Ceylon, China, Japan, and the Philippines.

Jim and Iva's wedding photo, 1913

Of course that was far from the end of my story. Iva and I had children together and shared some happy years. Although baseball didn't work out as well as I hoped, I still got to play for three different major-league teams. And when professional football started up, I was right there as a player and the president of the new American Football League that became the NFL. But all of that is another story and it is a long one. I guess you've heard enough about old Jim Thorpe for now. May your path be bright, my friends.

AUTHOR'S NOTE

Jim Thorpe has been one of my heroes ever since I can remember. I grew up at a time when there were few modern American Indian heroes. It was the era of "cowboys and Indians" in the movies and on TV, with the Indians usually the villains. Even the few "good Indians" were usually played by white actors. Jim Thorpe, though, was real. Even though the time of his great success was when my grandparents were young, his name still shone brighter than anyone else's. People spoke of him in the way I've heard Lakotas talk about Crazy Horse. Bigger than life. Legendary.

I admired the fact that Jim Thorpe had been a great football player on an all-Indian team and an Olympic gold medal winner who became known as the world's greatest athlete. I appreciated even more that he was a Sac and Fox Indian from Oklahoma who never forgot his roots. He not only always stayed close to his relatives and often went back home, he also remembered that what he gained from his success was meant to be shared. I can't count how many people have told me tales of his generosity, sometimes giving so much away that he made himself poor. Jim was what white people call "an easy touch," and what Indians call a man of heart.

I'd seen the movie about Jim (with Burt Lancaster in the title role) in which Jim was played as a sort of innocent. And I knew that his gold medals had been taken from him because he'd played baseball for money before going to the Olympic Games. But that didn't make Jim shine any less bright in my young eyes. Even back then, in my teenage years, I felt there was more to Jim's story than the Hollywood portrayal and the fall of a sports idol.

I never met Jim Thorpe, who passed on when I was only eleven years old. But later in life, as an adult, I was fortunate enough to meet people who'd been close to Jim and had their own stories about him to share. My friend and mentor Swift Eagle worked with Jim in Hollywood and taught me a Sac and Fox song that Jim gave him. Then there was Wendell Mt. Pleasant, brother of the same Frank Mt. Pleasant who not only played quarterback at Carlisle during Jim's first varsity year but also went to the Olympic Games and was second only to Jim as an all-around athlete. Wendell's stories of Frank and Jim in those Carlisle days really made them come alive for me.

It was then, a decade ago, that the idea first began to come to me about turning Jim Thorpe's story into a book for young readers. I read extensively and researched intensively, and found, quite frankly, that there were lots of mistakes and half-truths in many of the books written about Jim Thorpe—from his actual date of birth to statistics about his sports achievements. After a good deal of cross-checking, looking into primary sources, and relying on Jim Thorpe's family, I feel I've managed to avoid repeating some of those mistakes. I was fortunate enough along the way to get help from such generous folks as Barbara Landis, the Carlisle Indian School biographer of the Cumberland County Historical Society. Barbara—you are the best. I also received invaluable assistance from members of Jim's own family—especially Grace Thorpe. It was Grace (with the help, of course, of many others) who spent decades working to redeem her father's reputation. In 1982 his name was finally returned to the Olympic record books, and a year later replicas of his Olympic gold medals (the originals having been lost) were returned to his family, thirty years after his death. Her efforts also resulted in her father being memorialized on a Wheaties box in 2001. Robert L. Whitman, whose book *Jim Thorpe, Athlete of the Century*, is a wonderful pictorial biography of Jim Thorpe, was equally helpful.

The first result of my research and writing was, to be honest, not this book. It was a picture book called *Jim Thorpe's Bright Path*, illustrated by S. D. Nelson, one of my favorite artists. S.D. is Lakota and, like me, he grew up immersed in the Thorpe legend. I'm proud of that book, but it only went as far as Jim's being accepted onto the Carlisle football squad. I felt that there was a lot more to tell. I also knew that I wanted Jim's voice to be heard. I'd read his letters and the texts of some of his talks. To write a story that would give him space to be heard, I'd need to do another book, a long first-person telling.

Although I have novelized Jim's story by writing it

in his voice, this book is not fiction. I have not made up either any events in Jim's life or changed anything in terms of when and where things happened. Much of the dialogue is taken from research—words recorded as having been said by Jim and the other characters. And there are no fictional characters in this story. Every person I've named really lived and is reported to have said and done what I recount in this story.

I'd also like to add that this is not just another book about a sports hero, but deals with many issues that are still with us today. There's the difficult matter of amateur status. What is the line between the big-time college athlete and the pro and how does the influx of cash from sports affect education? Then there are also such big issues that still affect Native Americans, as the loss of language and culture, the unequal relationship with a dominant society, the problems of racism and stereotyping. It's my hope that Jim Thorpe's story will help people to understand a bit more about the long history of all of these problems and, perhaps, to think more clearly about what might be done in the future to address them.

AFTER CARLISLE

This novel ends with Jim embarking on a career in professional sports. Rather than just leave the reader there, here are a few words about what happened to Jim, Carlisle, Pop Warner, and some of the other Indian athletes who were Jim's friends and teammates.

In 1914 Carlisle had another great football year

266

with Gus Welch as their captain, winning ten and losing only one. But it was the last of their great years. The faculty and students finally decided they'd had enough. The way Jim had been used as a scapegoat was a big part of it. Gus Welch put together a petition complaining about mismanagement of the school. It ended up with those congressional hearings. Students and faculty members alike told of the brutal unjust punishments, the unfair expulsions, and the bad food the average students were given. At those hearings, Gus Welch testified about how Jim was one of those misused by Carlisle and how he had not composed that confession he was told to copy out in his own hand and sign.

Some of the biggest questions were about missing money that was supposed to have bought food, books, and supplies for the students or to have been kept in their accounts. This money had vanished, including the large sums that came in every year from the gate receipts at football games. Pop Warner refused to turn over his books and many of the records were conveniently lost.

When it was asked who the board members were of the Carlisle Athletic Association, it turned out that Mr. Sullivan of the AAU was one of them. His name was tarred along with everyone else's. Perhaps the investigation had nothing to do with it, but Sullivan died of a heart attack in September of that year. No one was ever convicted of any criminal offenses, but Superintendent Friedman left under a cloud and went on to run a School for Defective Boys in New Mexico.

Pop Warner coached his Indians one more year. It was his worst season ever. When the University of Pittsburgh offered Warner a job in 1915, after beating Carlisle 45–0, he accepted. Warner went on to coach at Pittsburgh for ten years, with three undefeated seasons, and then spent eight years at Stanford, where his record included winning three Rose Bowls. In 1934, he began leading clinics for kids and their coaches that developed into Pop Warner Football, an international youth football program that involves over 350,000 young people each year in the game Pop loved. Its aims are "to inspire youth, regardless of race, creed, religion, or national origin, to practice sportsmanship, scholarship, and physical fitness . . ." (My own two sons were Pop Warner Football players.) One of the winningest coaches in college football history, Pop Warner died of throat cancer in 1954.

Gus Welch, who had been working as an assistant coach at the time, took over the reins in the few years of Carlisle football that followed. He graduated from the Dickinson School of Law in 1917. Gus then volunteered for the army, became a captain, and served with distinction in Europe during World War I leading a troop of African-American engineers. He married Julia Carter (the congressman's daughter) in 1923 and went on to coach and teach physical education at Haskell, American University, Washington State, the

celebrity, athlete, and lecturer were cited as reasons for their split.

Indeed, much of Jim Thorpe's life after Carlisle was spent on the road. During the 1930s, like many other Americans, Jim and his family suffered from the Great Depression and Jim sometimes had to find jobs as a house painter and construction worker after his playing days were done. He also spent time in Hollywood between 1929 and the end of the 1930s in a new career that saw him playing parts in such MGM films as *Battling with Buffalo Bill, She,* and *The Green Light.* At one point he was in charge of all the Indian extras in Hollywood. Jim also was on the lecture circuit, speaking about sportsmanship, the American Indian today, and his own life story. He spoke at high schools and service clubs all over the United States, but he was often paid only a pittance.

When World War II began, Jim tried to enlist, even though he was fifty-seven years old by then. Rejected for service at first, he stubbornly persisted. He was finally allowed to join the Merchant Marines and served on a cargo ship transporting ammunition. In 1945, he married an old friend, Patricia Askew, who helped Jim get back on the lecture circuit for fees that were more respectable. It was said that even in his sixties, Jim could still punt a football the length of the field. But his health was not good. One bright spot of his last years was 1950, when the first of many honors—all too many of the rest posthumous—came his way. He was named the greatest football player of the first half of the century by an Associated Press poll. Jim was also paid $15,000 by MGM, which was making the story of his life: *Jim Thorpe—All-American*. On March 28, 1953, Jim died of a massive heart attack, his third.

Jim Thorpe, Original All-American

In 1954, the year after his death, the Jim Thorpe Trophy for the NFL's Most Valuable Player was instituted. In that same year the town of Mauch Chunk, Pennsylvania, where he was buried, was renamed Jim Thorpe, Pennsylvania. In 1963 Jim was enshrined in the Professional Football Hall of Fame in Canton, Ohio, where he'd played for the Bulldogs.

There's one more footnote to add. The story of Carlisle as an Indian school came to an end in 1918. The army decided it needed the Carlisle campus as a hospital for the wounded coming back from World War I in France. The flag was lowered on September 1, 1918 and the Carlisle Barracks became U.S. Army Base Hospital No. 31.

BIBLIOGRAPHY

The following bibliography does not include all the resources I used in writing this book. Instead, it is a list of what I consider the best and most accurate sources for anyone interested in learning more about Jim Thorpe, Carlisle, and the American Indian athletic tradition.

Bloom, John. *To Show What an Indian Can Do, Sports at Native American Boarding Schools*. Minneapolis: University of Minnesota Press, 2000. A brief, readable book that explores the history of sports programs at the U.S. Indian schools of the late nineteenth century and first half of the twentieth century, drawing on the recollections of former students.

Crawford, Bill. *All American: The Rise and Fall of Jim Thorpe*. Hoboken, NJ: John Wiley & Sons, Inc. 2005. This new book is lively and well researched. I consider it the best written historical treatment of Jim Thorpe thus far and I recommend it enthusiastically.

Newcombe, Jack. *The Best of the Athletic Boys: The White Man and Jim Thorpe*. New York: Doubleday, 1975. A colorfully written book that explores the complicated relationship between Jim Thorpe and the majority culture that shaped so much of his life.

Oxendine, Joseph B. *American Indian Sports Heritage*. Champaign, IL: Human Kinetics Books, 1988. A thorough and informative survey of American Indian sports, from the pre-Columbian past through most of the twentieth century. Oxendine, himself a Lumbee Indian, does an excellent job of proving how deeply American Indian games and Native athletes influenced and continue to affect American sports.

Wheeler, Robert W. *Jim Thorpe, World's Greatest Athlete*. Norman, OK: University of Oklahoma Press, 1981. Regarded by many as the most informative book about Jim Thorpe and his athletic career. Its author was the founder of the Jim Thorpe Foundation, a major force in restoring Thorpe's Olympic records.

Whitman, Robert L. *Jim Thorpe, Athlete of the Century, a Pictorial Biography*. Defiance, OH: Robert L. Whitman in Cooperation with the Jim Thorpe Society, 2002. No other book has as many photos of Jim, and the essays that describe the various stages of his life are succinct and informative. A great resource for school libraries.

————. *Jim Thorpe and the Oorang Indians, N.F.L.'s Most Colorful Franchise*. Defiance, OH: Robert L. Whitman in Cooperation with the Marion County Historical Society, 1984. The main focus of this book is the pro football team that Jim Thorpe founded, coached, and played for, but it also contains information about Jim's entire life and it places the Oorang Indians in context. Lots of photos, including individual shots of each of the American Indian players.

Witmer, Linda. *The Indian Industrial School, Carlisle, Pennsylvania, 1879–1918*. Carlisle, PA: Cumberland Historical Society, 1993. Filled with archival photos of the place and its students, as well as clear descriptions of many aspects of the school's history, this is the best book to give you a sense of life at Carlisle.

Best Bet on the Internet: Search the Carlisle Indian Industrial School Research Pages, which include sections on History, Jim Thorpe, a Virtual Tour, Biographies, and Related Links.

ABOUT THE AUTHOR

Joseph Bruchac is the author of more than 100 books, ranging from collections of his own poetry and retellings of traditional Native American tales to short stories and historical novels. His work as a storyteller and writer, which frequently reflects his Abenaki Indian ancestry, has won critical praise and numerous awards, including a Rockefeller Humanities fellowship, a National Endowment for the Arts poetry fellowship, the Cherokee Nation Prose Award, the Knickerbocker Award, a Lifetime Achievement Award from the Native Writers Circle of the Americas, and the Virginia Hamilton Literary Award.